Harmonize Your Home and Office,
and Feel more Alive

Diana Anderson

Written and developed by Diana Anderson

Ketchum, Idaho

Copyright © 2013 Diana Anderson

ISBN 978-0-9853307-5-0

Published by Words as My Wings, LLC

P.O. Box 6071

Ketchum, Idaho 83340

All Rights Reserved

First Edition 2013

Printed in the United States of America

1 3 5 7 9 10 8 6 4 2

Contents

Forward:

Like many people, I struggled with health issues. After numerous accidents and injuries, from sports to traffic accidents, my body had aches and pains. The American diet didn't support me in feeling well either. I was fortunate to receive The Reconnection© and learn how to meditate regularly with its frequency. Over a one year period of meditating, every pain in my body was gone. The only major issues remaining were my digestion and irregular heartbeats. Those would take years and many dietary improvements. After removing refined sugar and GMO foods from my diet, I finally went to a plant based diet. It took that dramatic change to really heal my digestion.

It didn't matter how healthy I became, I was still affected by the energy in buildings. Stale air, mold, lack of sunlight and florescent lighting could affect me even after all of my deep relaxation and mending.

I know my body. I notice a remarkable improvement in my mood, breathing and overall vitality when I am outdoors surrounded by the natural world. I long to feel that same lift of energy, while I'm indoors.

One day I was meditating on the idea of geometry. I saw clear, vivid images of what Plato called the platonic solids, which are patterned measurements inside the earth. I could see that what effects one area of our planet creates effects across the globe as the grid of symmetrical shapes span the earth and connect the whole. I noted that the earth was similar to our bodies; if one area is sick, it weakens the rest.

We are destroying the rain forest, polluting the oceans, treating animals as objects, and valuing money over quality of life. It is deplorable. In addition to the moral ramifications there are the physical effects on ourselves. It behooves us to respect our planet, which provides one hundred percent of our resources. When we neglect caring for Mother Earth, we mistreat our own bodies. What happens to her, impacts us.

Homes and buildings are an extension of the earth and a way for us to live within the shelter that earth's resources provide. The builders of buildings have the opportunity to respect the earth by honoring nature and animals in the process of design and construction, creating structures that are compatible with the resonate frequencies of fresh air, clean water and earth's rhythms. We can all do our part to support building as an extension of nature.

When we are in harmony with the planet, and our homes and buildings are in harmony, we thrive and feel more alive!

1 Harmony is Contagious

When the universe is in harmony with man, the eternal, we know it as truth, but we feel it as beauty.

~Tagore

November 2006 was the first time that I touched the infinite and merged with all that is. I floated in a sea of bliss without edges and experienced the deepest peace of my entire life. This happened to me during a session of The Reconnection, which is a hands-off healing modality that balances the energy field of the body and connects the body's field to every other field in the universe.

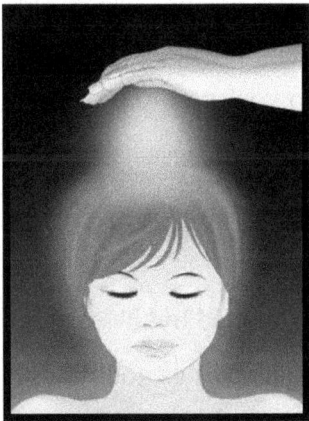

Two months after I received The Reconnection[1], I began to change significantly. The things that used to be important to me; money, clients, recognition, and reputation, faded away. New priorities dominated my time; family, friends, fun, creativity. I opened my mind and heart and the universe began to whisper to me.

---

[1] www.thereconnection.com

Quiet whispers let me know that nothing caresses the senses as well as harmony. Art, great movies, beautiful music, people working well together, room colors balancing each other, musicians jamming in rhythm and dance teams stepping in sync are just a few of the ways the human senses are stroked by unity.

There are many ways to create harmony in your life. The more ways you experience harmony, the more ways you will improve your experience. When your environment is harmonious, you are more relaxed.

Nature is brilliant at creating this sensation. I love to spend time in nature because it *feels so good.* The forest sings in rhythmic pulsation with trees, animals, plants and birds all resonating together. Night creatures such as crickets, frogs, owls, and bats, synchronize like a well-conducted orchestra. You resonate with this feeling because you are intricately related to nature's tempo. How strong is your connection with the planet? Are you aware of her rhythms? Do you do your part to protect her resources and the lives of the animals, plants, insects and people who depend on her? Your relationship with the earth is a direct reflection of your self-respect.

Do you breathe well in nature, surrounded by the earth's natural pulses, which beat at the same frequencies as your body? These frequencies can soothe and comfort you.

Buildings have a different pace than nature. Compare how you feel spending eight hours in an office building without windows or fresh air, verses the day at the park for a family picnic or a long hike. It feels different inside an office building than it does in a park, just as it feels different to spend time in the mountains than it does to be in a large metropolitan city. The variations in frequency patterns are noticeable.

"Earthing" is a new buzz word that many people are talking about, even Dr. Oz. "Earthing" means being grounded to the earth. Science is learning that we are healthier when we spend time connected and grounded with our planet. [2] You and I benefit from natural sunlight, fresh air and contact with plants and animals. Walking barefoot on the beach or grass or walking through a park or forest path is highly beneficial to your health. Water trickling over rocks, or waves running up the beach, releases negative ions that nourish and support the human body.

Being aware of the moon cycles, the seasons, and watching the birds migrate and respond to the environment helps to bring you into balance and harmony with the earth. When you are in coherence with nature, your own rhythms regulate; including your parasympathetic nervous system. Your heart beat is more relaxed, oxygen and blood flow and your breathing is more productive when your body feels in tune with natural world.

Take a moment to recognize how you feel walking on the beach along the ocean, strolling on a path in the forest, swimming

---

[2] Dr. Oz on Earthing http://www.foodrenegade.com/earthing-on-dr-oz/

in a lake, viewing wildlife, stroking your cat or dog or watching a hummingbird drink nectar. What are you feeling when the sunshine is bathing you and a soft breeze is caressing your face, or a small puppy is licking your fingers and then you watch it bouncing at play? Now compare those feelings to entering a school, an office building, or a gym.

The vibration of nature is slower than that of electronics and lighting in buildings. Your body feels relaxed when surrounded by the slower vibrations. I can sit around a campfire with friends for hours mesmerized by the glowing flames and chat until way past my bedtime. Sometimes I park myself by a lake to sunbathe or watch my sweetheart fish. The day could pass away while I rest there content as can be. But if I am in an airport with a two hour layover, I can't wait to be somewhere else. I feel that I am wasting my time, and there are many places I would rather be. The intense vibrations in airports make me feel rushed, and I want to move fast. In nature I feel relaxed, as if I want to stop and soak up what is around me.

What causes the difference?

Buildings are quite valuable. They protect people from the weather. They provide comfort, safety, security and privacy. Yet ideally, they also should feel harmonious to us.

Our human body synchronizes with frequency patterns around us, whether they are produced by the earth's magnetic field or the sound of a rock band. Your normal heart and brain rhythms match the frequency pattern generated between the surface of the earth and the ionosphere. This frequency is known as the Schumann Resonance. It was discovered by the German physicist Winfried Otto Schumann. [3]

The Schumann Resonance helps maintain natural human rhythms, such as hormone production, melatonin level, menstrual and sleep cycles. Astronauts became ill and unable to sleep in space while deprived of this vital frequency. Dr. Wolfgang Ludwig of Germany, known as the Father of Magnetic Therapy, convinced NASA to install the "Schumann Simulator," a magnetic pulse generator to mimic the Earth's frequency, and all shuttles are now equipped with this life balancing device to protect the health and life of the astronauts. [4]

---

[3] http://en.wikipedia.org/wiki/Schumann_resonances
http://www.glcoherence.org/monitoring-system/earth-rhythms.html
http://sedonanomalies.weebly.com/schumann-resonance.html
[4] http://ntrs.nasa.gov/archive/nasa/casi.ntrs.nasa.gov/201200 00051_2011023798.pdf

You can experience the same symptoms here on earth as the astronauts did in space when you do not receive this healthy earth frequency. To some degree, most modern buildings interrupt the Schumann Resonance and produce conflicting frequencies. The Schumann Resonance is disrupted by metal wiring, metal roofs, or the rebar used in reinforced concrete. A high-rise structure with thousands of pounds of wiring, computer equipment and electronic appliances generates a higher hertz than the Schumann Resonance.

Industrial plants or prisons, built from tons of reinforced concrete, disrupt this frequency from flowing in the structure, preventing the people inside from receiving enough of this life-force. These higher frequencies, generated by the electric currents and wireless transmissions, interfere with the natural vibrations so vital to human health. When you lack resonance with the natural rhythm of the earth's frequencies, you feel drained, have headaches and experience negative emotions as your biorhythms become aligned with the building's frequency instead of the earth's.

Another frequency that influences our bodies is the earth's magnetic field that is part of the polarity of north and south. This field is also very healing to the human body. Metals that interrupt the Schumann Resonance, interfere with this field as well. Just as a wireless internet signal is interrupted by wiring, metal and conflicting frequencies, so is the earth's *wireless transmissions*.

Electrical wiring, reinforced concrete and large amounts of metal are new environments for humans to dwell within. For most of the duration of humanity, we lived outdoors and the structures we built consisted of natural materials without electric currents and wireless transmissions such as internet, television, radio and satellite. It has only been in the last one hundred years that human bodies have been subjected to new and constantly changing frequencies that were absent in most of our evolution. Certainly people are adapting, but at what price? As we progress I will share with you how you can make your buildings compatible with your body and the earth.

The feeling of relaxation and harmony that you experience in nature can be created indoors by *reconnecting* the rhythms in your buildings with the natural frequency of the earth and our atmosphere. I learned how to remedy these frequency incompatibility issues and I will teach you how to build a grid to reconnect the Schumann Resonance and earth's magnetic field to your home and work place.

The word reconnect is not uncommon in our everyday world. People say that they want to reconnect with an old friend. Lovers want to reconnect with their original passion, a therapist wants a client to reconnect with their inner child, or you might choose to reconnect with family traditions. Connecting and reconnecting are part of life. Here I will apply the meaning as follows: to reconnect the energy in buildings with the natural rhythms of our planet and atmosphere. Literally the field of the building harmonizes with the magnetic field of the planet.

I will also teach you how to create a spiral to balance the magnetic field. With these vital frequencies in place, you will be surrounded by the vibrations needed to improve your well-being.

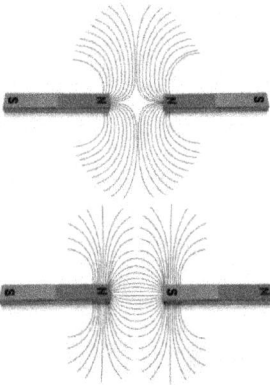

Products have been introduced in the marketplace that people can wear to mimic this type of magnetic field around a person and support the human body. There are Schumann Resonance devices of many types available for purchase on the Internet, all of which try to imitate the natural resonance. You can also create this field around yourself anytime you want, naturally, without wearing a device. I will teach you how.

Do you pay attention to how you feel from one setting to another? I suggest that you notice how a building's vibrations makes you feel in contrast to how another space feels, or how an outdoor area affects you. When you pay close attention, you will notice that your own body's vibrations might shift to match the vibrations of your surroundings. You also adjust to the vibrations of people around you, such as members of your family, friends and co-workers. Have you observed that when you spend time with co-workers you behave differently than you do when you are with your family? Your vibrations shift, depending on who you are with, and where you are. For example, you feel differently in a doctor's office than you do in a bar.

When I am with my girlfriend Karen, we can talk about anything and everything. But when I am with my friend Janet, the conversation is more conservative. Janet and Karen have different vibrations, which translates into unique belief systems and personalities. When I spend time with my daughters, I am different than when I am spending time in a professional setting. This might be called, "what is appropriate in society," but the truth is it all stems from the vibration generated by the situation and the people involved. The vibration in buildings affects you in a similar way. You shift with your surroundings.

However, I can show you how to stand firm in your own resonance and not allow people and structures to change your balance. When you are grounded solid in your rhythms, you feel well and function naturally in any environment.

Noticing when a home or office makes you feel uncomfortable or ill is helpful to improve your experiences. A good sign that a building is out of harmony with the planet is if you cannot wait to leave the premises and never wish to return.

Have you noticed how you feel when you enter a large retail store lit by florescent light, with concrete walls? Does the energy feel like it is moving fast in crazy patterns? When I visit certain retail locations, I feel an annoying buzz at my temples within a short time after entering. My body feels stressed and I cannot wait to leave. In the stores where I feel the worst, I frequently hear a young child screaming. No doubt the child is sensitive to unnatural environment.

This feeling is quite different from how you might feel when you lie down in the grass bathed in sunshine. You wish that you could stay there all day. Or how you feel when you are on a walk in nature at lunch. In nature you might be thinking, "I wish I didn't have to go back to the office."

Connecting a building to the Schumann Resonance, and strengthening the magnetic field of the building, will help people feel better inside of the edifice. It may or may not address all of the vibrational issues such as emotional frequencies caused by the people who occupy the space. Business practices and policies may not be helped by the Schumann Resonance. For example, if the business has a policy of getting the most out of their customer's pockets, or a restaurant serves low quality food, then the natural frequencies may not shift that energy. That is where programming comes in handy, which I will teach in later chapters. However, if a business has a policy of treating the customer well, that too will positively affect the energy of the building, in addition to the natural frequencies.

There is a small local grocery store near my house which I frequent. They focus on quality and support local, organic growers and fair trade. It is more expensive, yet I've noticed that the atmosphere is welcoming, supportive, healthy and relaxed. I have never heard a child screaming in this store. At two areas in the store there are posters explaining local events. You can place your business card and flyer on the bulletin board at the back of the store. The store is small, but the atmosphere supports people and well-being.

The owners and employees of this store have the intention of being in balance with the planet and supporting human health on all levels. Their intentions have an impact on how it feels inside the business.

For ten years I sold commercial buildings as a real estate professional, and evaluated the worth of hundreds of homes and buildings. I often noticed that each building had its own unique atmosphere and each impacted me a little differently. I also noticed that some buildings had frequent turnover because a business just could not survive in that space, no matter what business tried to make it. In these situations the building usually had energy problems and didn't support a business in a healthy manner. This may seem impossible to consider, but most likely you have walked into a building that didn't feel good to you. If a business is located in one of these buildings, employees suffer, customers do not return and business falters.

You always have the ability to allow a space to affect you in a positive, even if the space is not grounded. By bringing yourself to full awareness, completely present, you can decide to be in the experience fully conscious, instead of impacted by the "music" around you that you don't enjoy. I will share more about how to be present and grounded in the following chapters.

Personal Experience

As a child I lived in the foothills above downtown Boise, Idaho. The homes were built on the foothill rims, leaving the valleys and slopes of the land wild and open. I spent my free time playing in these vast hills with my sister and friends. We walked on trails that wound around the curving ridges. We built forts in the hillsides, caught grasshoppers, and walked a mile down the hill to the corner store for candy. I experienced my favorite childhood memories there.

I decided to move my own family closer to downtown to be near friends and activities. I was naturally drawn back to the foothills of my happy childhood. A new phase of building lots just happened to be available. My youngest daughter and I walked on several building sites, paying attention to the view and how we felt on each lot before we selected the one we liked best.

A professional home designer carefully drew plans to take advantage of the view. I spent many months choosing all the right colors, materials, finishes and features. The results were my dream home; bold and artistic, yet warm and inviting. It incorporated a modern motif with a Zen flare and rich colors. Aesthetically it turned out better than I envisioned. Finally our dream home was completed and we moved in feeling gratitude and elation.

The first day in our new home was Saturday. As we went about our day unpacking, I noticed a new pattern emerging. All four of us experienced a rollercoaster of emotional swings. One minute we felt ecstatic, the next irritable. I wondered if it might be the stress of moving.

"Rachael, how are you feeling?" I asked my oldest daughter.

"It's kinda funny," she said, "one minute I'm excited to be here and minutes later I'm edgy and frustrated. I don't know what's going on."

"Does it feel like the house is irritating you in some way?" I asked her.

She paused and crinkled her nose. "Yeah, that's right…it feels like this place is not natural to me or comfortable, even though I want to be here."

"I know, me too," I said.

I consulted my boyfriend, Dan, and my youngest daughter, Jasmine. Dan thought that moving caused us to be stressed. We all agreed that something affected our moods. I decided my new home needed immediate balancing, harmonizing and connecting to natural frequencies.

On Sunday I built a grid according to the steps I had used previously to balance and connect the homes of friends and clients. I went through the process and implemented all of the steps that I will teach you throughout this book. It worked. Immediately we had a shift in the energy and my entire family felt it. We stopped having the sweeping mood swings we felt the day before. The balancing, however, still was not complete.

The next day, Monday, I asked my two daughters, "How do you feel today, girls?"

Rachael spoke up first, "I feel kinda sick."

"What do you mean?"

"Just a slight headache and nausea," she explained.

"And you Jasmine?"

"The same, mostly nausea, but a little headache too," she said holding her hand over her stomach.

"I feel it too," I told my daughters. "Well, I'm new at the balancing thing. I'll try it again today."

At first I wondered if the cause of our symptoms was from the chemicals in all the new materials. I sat quietly, cleared my thoughts and doubts, and centered myself in my heart. I paid attention to how the energy felt to me. As I sat quietly, in my body I experienced the sensation of instability. In my mind's eye I saw a tall pillar standing but not anchored by anything, as if it

14

might topple over any minute. The instability in the energy was making us ill.

I had balanced a few spaces over the past months, but had not encountered this problem before. I was not sure what to do.

While I was sitting quietly I felt a strong impression that the energy needed to rotate inside the structure in a spiral, clockwise going up and counterclockwise going down, from the center point of the home. This would support the magnetic field.

I received a visual image of a snail shell spiral. As I followed the intuitive steps to create a spiral, I felt a clean, rushing new energy fill me and engulf me. Afterwards I felt light and fresh.

By Wednesday, my new home felt secure and peaceful. My family and I were very pleased. We were relaxed and cheerful. New guests commented that our home felt wonderful and welcoming. Even though the shifts in energy were subtle, they were powerful.

The most important and effective activity that I did was becoming completely present with my home. The ritual provided a way for me to continue to stay present and feel the space. Listening with my heart, feeling with my body and interacting with the energy, was what caused the shift to occur. What I saw and felt in my mind's eye and body was my interpretation of the experience mixed with my understanding of earth's energy fields.

You can connect a space, or better said, connect with a space, in a way that works well for you. You can use my grid technique, and ritual, or you can find your own way to interact with the space and clear the imbalances. You have a powerful magnetic field around your body. When your field is grounded, you influence the spaces around you.

Many native people used burning sage for hundreds of years to clear imbalanced energy. The intention and the focus are the essential ingredients.

Establishing harmonious energy in my home was a giant step for me in recognizing my own power to affect my world and the quality of my experience here. I wondered, *If I can make such a sudden and profound effect in my home, how else can I affect the energy around me?* As I pondered this idea, more insight came to me about my power to change energy patterns in all areas of my life. The common denominator was being fully present.

Obviously, when you feel well at work, you are more productive. If you feel well at home, you are kinder to your family. Once the environment in my home shifted to harmony, I found more time for connecting with my deeper-self and to enjoy more tranquility.

At Christmas my daughters confirmed my feeling that I was more at peace. All of my daughters were at my home to celebrate the holiday. Rachael, Jenny and Jasmine, as well as Jenny's new husband Jay were sitting in the living room, near the tree, with Dan and me. During a casual conversation, my oldest daughter Rachael said, "Mom, you are so much happier. It's fun to see this new you." "Yeah," Jenny said nodding, "It's so true." Jasmine nodded "yes" as well. I knew that I felt better, and it was rewarding to realize my girls noticed it also.

Learning to control my thoughts gave me control over my own happiness. Living in harmony with the earth and The Schumann Resonance, helped me create harmony all around me. Respecting all things on the planet allowed me to see my own abundance. Each day I move within a space of appreciation, love, peace and harmony. This shift was made by choice.

There was no doubt that the shift was helpful for all of us. But then I wondered…*How far can I take this? What are all of the benefits from reconnecting buildings?*

2 Our Modern Landscape

We shape our buildings; thereafter they shape us.
~Winston Churchill.

Buildings are ecosystems where people, pets, and bugs coincide.
~Diana Anderson

Here is a typical scenario: Jenny is a thirty five year old, single mom of three daughters, who wakes up each day in her suburbia home outside of Seattle, Washington. She works eight-hours in a medical billing office, frequents her neighborhood grocery store as well as the dry cleaners, plus attends her oldest daughter's bi-weekly basketball practice at the school gym.

Jenny works in a large room filled with small cubicles, florescent lighting and no windows. Around 11:00 am each day she begins to feel her shoulders tighten. After lunch she fights fatigue for most of the afternoon. By three or four o'clock she experiences irritability and withdraws from her co-workers to avoid being snappy with them or experiencing their end-of-the-day grumpiness. In the grocery store Jenny often feels over stimulated. While picking up her dry cleaning her body tenses just a little while she breathes shallow. The loud screeches, thumps, and screams at the gym irritate her head and nerves. At home she feels safe, and more comfortable, yet never able to stop to rest because of endless incomplete tasks. The vibration of the buildings Jenny visits impact her mental, emotional and physical well-being.

Have you ever walked into a basement without windows and felt uncomfortable? Reinforced concrete obstructs the many frequencies that benefit your physical systems. Without these essential elements, you will not feel well, which is the body's way of telling us that the space is lacking in the frequencies you need. Places where people live or work, that are constructed of reinforced concrete walls, or have high amounts of electrical and computer wiring, require the human system to make large adjustments from what is natural. The World Health Organization[5] recognizes that many office and industrial work environments have high rates of complaints; headaches, fatigue, sleepiness, irritation to eyes and nose, dry throat, general loss of concentration, lethargy, dizziness, irritability, forgetfulness and nausea.

The inanimate buildings around you are also forms of

---

[5] Sick Building Syndrome is a term used when people become ill or have adverse symptoms because of working in a building that makes them sick. This is considered a serious issue today. http://en.wikipedia.org/wiki/Sick_building_syndrome

energy. Everything is made of energy and buildings are a composite of many different energies working together. They have a magnetic field, energy flow and a life-force. They are all part of the same energy is in our make-up. Every atom has a magnetic field. Buildings are a large compilation of atoms, creating one big magnetic field.

You develop a relationship with a building much like you do with people. These relationships are similar to your human associations in that they can feel healthy and uplifting or negative and depleting. People often select their homes based on how it makes them feel. The frequency of a building can impact you as soon as you walk inside because of synchronization.

In the sixteenth century synchronization came to light by a Dutch physicist and inventor, Christian Huygens[6]. He called it entrainment and it simply means that two things left together synchronize their vibrations to the strongest rhythm of the two.

A good way to think about this is how you entrain with the music and beats around you. Think about how certain music makes you feel. What if you listen to Reggae? How do you feel listening to rock? How about Hip Hop, Country, Jazz, Tribal, Indian, Hawaiian, acoustical and so on? Different music affects you in unique ways because of the diverse vibrations of the

---

[6] https://en.wikipedia.org/wiki/Entrainment_(physics)

music. Various vibrations of people and places also affect you in a variety of ways.

Recently I attended an activity called a Spirit Dance. As a participant, I was blind folded and was encouraged to dance my spirit as I listened to the different rhythms. The instruments included several flutes, drums, rattles, and a didgeridoo. There was also an instrument to mimic the ocean and one that sounded like thunder. As I danced with the blindfold in place and focused on expressing the music through my body, I noticed that each instrument had a slightly different effect on the way my body felt, and how I moved. When the drums were dominant my body felt active, moved fast, felt energized, firm and strong. When the flutes were prominent, my body felt soft, moved slowly, felt restful and at peace. The rattles seemed to stimulate every cell in my body to move. The ocean waves and thunder grounded me and brought me back to an appreciation for earth. With the didgeridoo I felt like a tree, firmly planted in the earth with a quiet mind and a slow pace.

Life is playing music all around you every day. The vibration of the traffic, air conditioners, computers, dishwashers, telephone, lights and radio are all singing a tune that impacts how you feel. Buildings are full of vibrations and they all play a song.

When you walk into a building and you are not centered and balanced, then you could entrain your rhythm with that of the building and occupants. This happens when office workers entrain with the flicking florescent lights, computers and hums of equipment around them and they become tired, irritable and are taxed with other physical symptoms. Women's menstrual cycles do the same thing. The strongest vibrational wave engulfs the others. Picture ripple waves in a pond from a stone tossed in the water. Now a child jumps into the pond and the effects from the child's splash take over the stone's ripples, which then become part of the larger undulation. The child's waves are stronger and overtake the smaller ones.

These patterns that we see throughout nature and the cosmos are universal. The Golden Mean and fractal geometry are the pattern of everything ever made that is not developed by man. Sometime man has copied this formula, Such as the Romans that built buildings using specific geometry shapes and sizes common in nature. DE Vinci understood these proportions and used them in his art.

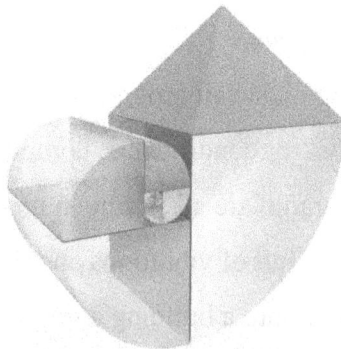

During the many millennia that humans existed on this planet, we entrained our systems to synchronize with the rhythm of the larger field (wave) of our home planet. Your body's biorhythms fall in the same frequency array as the earth's atmosphere and your eyes and heart are entrained to the pattern of creation, which is fractal geometry.

Even our atmosphere is a wave pattern of fractal geometry. When the astronauts left our atmosphere in the first space shuttle, they experienced difficulty sleeping, plus they suffered from similar issues that The World Health Organization hears about from office workers, because they were deprived of the Shuman Resonance which the body requires. [7]

---

[7] Schumann Resonators in the space shuttles
http://www.schumannresonator.com/
http://www.granddistraction.com/schumann-resonance/
http://www.echad.se/echad-science-tuning/schumann-scale

The Schumann Resonance is a fluctuating fractal frequency generated between the surface of the earth and the ionosphere. It oscillates roughly between 6 and 60 hertz. The human heart, brain and biorhythms move within this same frequency range. Appliances and lighting, however, vary from 60 hertz to 500 hertz and up. Cell phones and computers are high in the range.

Inside a building you are exposed to frequencies much greater than your human body needs for optimal health. In certain work situations people become exposed to high frequency waves from many different sources. As the body tries to synchronize with these unnatural vibrations, it affects the body like high doses of caffeine or other foreign substances, draining the body of vitality. People working in these environments all day become exhausted as their bodies vibrate at the rhythms of the environment.

Reconnecting the vibrations of the buildings with the Schumann Resonance connects the energies together in a way that is harmonizing. Vibrations are like electricity that only needs a conduit to travel from one place to another. Reconnecting a building to the earth creates a path for the vibration of the earth to connect to the vibration of the building and occupants. You can establish the conduit between the building and nature.

The presence of the Schumann Resonance in a building allows for better air quality. Poor ventilation vibrates at a different frequency than fresh air, which vibrates with the earth's natural frequencies. Fresh mountain spring water has a different vibration than city tap water; as you can witness in Masaru Emoto's extensive work on the frequency of water.[8]

You are a conscious creator. You create all the time. You have the ability to affect the frequencies all around you. You can use your thoughts and beliefs to significantly improve your experience by being the stronger signal for the atmosphere in a building to entrain to. For example, collectively the country may have a belief that resources are scarce and limited. As long as the collective has this thought pattern, it will be what the collective people experience. As more and more believe in abundance, and a planet designed to supply everything needed when used with respect, the experience for all will improve.

The Institute of Heart Math[9] and the Global Coherence Initiative[10] have been studying the effects of our heart rhythms and thoughts as a collective people across the planet as well as the effects of the planet changes on our heart rhythms. They discovered that the overall thinking pattern of the masses can be measured in the ionosphere, because our conscious thinking appears to be directly linked to it. Instruments can measure the vibration of the collective people and even predict days, hours, or

---

[8] Shows how water responds to words, pictures, thoughts, and intention. http://www.masaru-emoto.net/english/water-crystal.html
[9] http://www.heartmath.org/
[10] http://www.glcoherence.org/

moments in advance when disaster is eminent in a specific region. The vibration of communities increases to a high level of stress, moments before a tragedy that will affect many: such as a tsunami, a terrorist attack or an earthquake. Their studies also showed that when a number of people meditate on peace in a given area, the region is positively affected; crime decreased and the area has more peace.

Since we are not going back to a world without satellites and internet, the human body will need to learn to adjust to the many new frequencies around us. We adjust by accepting and not resisting. Resistance causes friction, discomfort and pain. Acceptance creates harmony. When I find myself in a building that is not comfortable, I first make sure I am grounded in my own energy with a firm connection to the earth. That alone might be enough. If it is not, then after I am sure I am grounded, I merge my energy with the building and become present with it. My total acceptance removes any resistance between me and the vibration of the structure. Existing in harmony with the energy of the structure, there becomes a place inside of me that understands that the building is only energy. The discomfort is only energy. Energy can be transformed. Merging with the building grounds it to the earth, through me. I didn't reconnect the structure permanently, but I did temporarily, similarly to how an energy healer can ground another person.

Most buildings are sufficiently grounded to the earth through grounding wires, they have window and wood to allow in light and the Schumann Resonance and they have ways for fresh air to enter them. Most homes and many buildings already feel good to us and don't need to be more connected with earth energy. Some buildings, however, do need to be connected. How will you know if a building needs balance or to be connected? You will know by the way you feel inside of the structure. If a building makes you feel tense, or gives you a creepy, crawly, "you're not wanted here" energy, then the building's frequencies are not aligned with those in your body. If the building makes you tired or uncomfortable, chances are it needs to be connected. Frequencies impact your body and emotions. If you feel well, supported, energized, and as comfortable as if you were standing in nature, then the building is well balanced. If you want to leave, or it seems dingy, smelly, heavy, creepy, or you are uncomfortable physically, then you know that it is out of sync with the earth.

Another way to know if the building is resonating with the earth's rhythm is if it has fresh air, natural light, and a pleasant smell. If plants will not grow in the structure, then the earth's frequencies are absent or low. If it smells dusty, unpleasant and it is difficult to breathe or relax, then the frequencies need to be addressed.

Developing a plan for a better future

My eldest daughter Rachael graduated from college with her masters in architecture. She completed her thesis on affordable, attractive housing for low income families. In her thesis she shows photographs of people slumped over with their heads in their hands sitting on crumbling steps in un-kept yards. Deteriorating buildings and unhealthy designs impact the residences' spirit. The exterior and interior walls shown were constructed of concrete with very small windows which allow for only a tiny bit of natural light. Some of the apartments have windows that don't open. The rhythm of the energy shows on the faces of those who live there. The healthy frequencies are low and it impacts their body, mind and spirit.

Some low income housing was designed with little thought for the health and well-being of the occupants. The intention of the design was affordable shelter, not vitality. The materials used in the structures were chosen in an effort to save on costs. The designs fail to meet the basic needs of the human spirit. The frustration of the people is apparent, but they lack other options. Even the well-meaning idea of housing people is lost in the creation. In order to allow people to thrive we must choose material, layout and design carefully, respecting people, the planet and social interaction. It can be done the way my daughter's thesis speaks of, with future occupants helping in construction and maintenance to create a connection between occupant and structure. Habitat for Humanity is doing this very idea all over the world.

Buildings impact your health, your senses, the amount of natural light you experience, the amount of high frequency waves and natural waves that you are exposed to. Buildings impact the air you breathe. They allow certain sounds in and they expose you to different smells. They have various textures and temperatures. Their layout determines how you mingle with and meet others, or how easy or difficult it is to hear a conversation. Buildings influence your mental, physical and emotional states with their sensory stimulus. As a result, they influence your success at home and at work.

Everything in our world is composed of atoms, which are suspected to be vibrating strings of light at their core. A building is a compilation of untold numbers of atoms. Each atom has a magnetic field. The electromagnetic field helps to hold the atom in its pattern, so it doesn't decompose. If an atom loses its field, it disappears and becomes unorganized light. When a building has a strong magnetic force field, the structure is less susceptible to decay; or disappearing atoms. When we consciously pay attention to atoms, or are being present with them, it strengthens their field.

New studies show the health benefits of walking barefoot on the earth, getting direct and indirect sunlight, drinking clean water and breathing unpolluted air. You can, however, improve the energy in your buildings to enhance your health and happiness. You live in an environment of buildings, which makes it more challenging to connect with our planet, get enough vitamin D, fresh air and grounded frequency from the earth. People have asked me if connecting a structure can improve cooperation in a family sharing a home, help a building or home to sell quickly, remove stale energy left by previous owners or tenants, help a business thrive, or increase the joy, productivity and camaraderie in a place. I answer with this; anytime you create harmony, and instigate balance with the earth and nature, you will improve the way people feel. When people are comfortable in a space, at home or at work, they can thrive and find more success. Likewise, if they don't feel good in a space, disagreements may arise or health issues may surface. You can bring harmony to your everyday experiences. It begins with respect for your natural environment and for the structures that you occupy.

3 In the Zone

There were probably about five games in my career where everything was moving in slow motion and you could be out there all day, totally in the zone, and you don't even know where you are on the field, everything is just totally blocked out. ~Lawrence Taylor

When I feel like I'm doing my best work, there is a bit of a freedom, a bit of flight that you're not so much losing yourself but you're sort of in the zone. ~Chris Cooper

Q.) What gave Mozart the inspiration to play and Michael Angelo the talent to paint?

A) Their ability to create came from their power in the zone where creation of the new begins.

We are all creators; DJ's, singers, home makers, mothers, builders, tile setters and computer programmers. Have you ever had that experience where you feel that you move through your experience effortlessly, guided by some unseen force? Many athletes and artists report feeling this state when they are at the *top of their game.* In this place you stop resisting, fearing, and judging life and you just *be*. In this magical place you become flowing energy, going downstream with the current of life.

An artist that is *in the zone* paints her masterpiece, a musician composes his ballad, an athlete plays the game without thinking about it because he is in the flow. People report a heightened sense of awareness and guidance, taking in all of the energy around them, open to all possibilities. In the zone, you create moment to moment, without hesitation. You connect with your unlimited power while in the zone. By being present in the moment, fully aware, you have access to pure consciousness.

I have friends who ski and snowboard in the zone, or said another way, in the present moment. Everything else disappears as they float in a world of snow and bliss. On auto pilot, they flow with pure energy, creating ecstasy moment by moment as they make a turn, glide through deep powder and zoom past white capped trees. They tune into their creative power by following what they love from their heart.

Think of a time when you felt connected with pure energy and were able to do something with ease. This generally happens when you focus on a task, such as a jigsaw puzzle, a hike in nature, listen to music or do your favorite activity. You experience a heightened sense of focus and your efforts flow naturally. This feeling gives you the power to create.

The Reconnection uses a similar technique. The practitioner must be fully present with the receiving person. The practitioner is observing the person's subtle body movement and they are feeling the electromagnetic field of the receiving person. This take focused awareness. This concentration of being present allows for a magical shift to happen. I say magical because we don't really understand it. What I do know is that I healed my physical body by putting my full awareness on the areas that needed healed. Putting complete, present awareness causes energy to flow there and healing to happen. We can do the same things with buildings and locations.

This same present moment focus is required to connect a building. When I connect a building, I am in the zone. I am aware of my senses that feel the unseen world that exists all around us. I practice getting in the zone through meditation and focused awareness. I meditate, and do a specific breathing technique. I reach a certain point where breathing feels completely effortless, as if I am not breathing into my lungs, but my entire body is a breathing machine. I feel air pouring into my body through my skin as if I am being filled with life force without *doing* anything. I am tapped in to the magical zone by clearing my thoughts and being open; like a giant lung where I breathe in everything around me.

There are many ways to experience this space of being present. Your experience may be very different from mine. It is a place where thoughts are quiet and experiencing is your focus. Other ways may include:

- Sitting quietly beside a lake noticing the environment
- Holding a cat or small dog and petting it for an extended period of time
- Walking a dog in nature
- Hiking, biking, golf and other outdoor sports
- Needle point or focused crafts
- Competitive sports
- Gardening
- Meditation or yoga
- Cooking
- Lying in the grass or sitting by a river

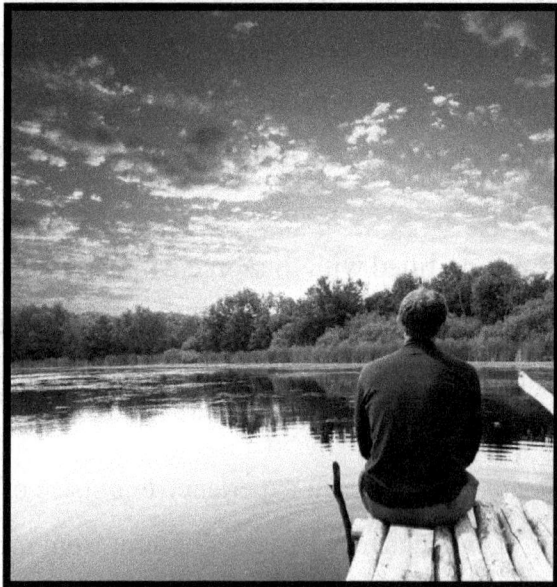

From this paranormal place I feel the vibrations from the buildings of our modern landscape. Tapping into this power, in the zone, I am able to make positive changes to the rhythms around me. I find the center of my heart and I send out a signal that could be called love, acceptance, awareness or oneness.

My ability to make changes begins in my imagination and I possess as much power as I find there. The only limits that exist for you and me are self-imposed. Your manifestation powers equal your perceived capacity along with the amount of energy you willingly put forth.

A composer friend of mine spends months imagining a sonnet before she brings it into form. The more time she spends using her imaginative skills, the more complete the manifestation. As she hears the music internally, she sends the vibrations out to manifest it into physical form. If she didn't believe that she could do it, then she couldn't. Likewise you must believe that you can create balanced energy in order to do so.

I use the following technique to get into *the zone* so that I know my own power to create balance around me. This method grounds my energy, and connects me to consciousness, the earth and my surroundings.

The Breathing Technique:

(Note: This technique is not something most people would learn in a day or two. It takes practice, like mastering any new activity.)

35

First I lie on my back or sit with my spine perfectly straight. I wiggle my body to adjust until my spine and head alignment feel straight. If you tend to fall asleep lying down, then do this while sitting up in a chair or on the floor with legs crossed. I relax my breathing to slow, rhythmic, deep, cleansing breaths. The intake is much slower than most people are used to. I breathe as if I am totally calm until my mind relaxes and my concerns melt away. This could take me one minute or up to thirty depending on the resistance of the mind to let go. The slow, focused breathing clears my mind. I intentionally expand my nostrils and trachea while simultaneously using my chest muscles to stretch my lungs gently open, not just up toward my throat, but outwards in all directions. The entire chest cavity and belly enlarges. I picture my lungs expanding, making room for air, as I slowly take in oxygen. As my chest swells, it allows air to pour into my lower and upper lungs. I do not suck the air in or pull it in. I open my airways and feel them filling with air. One breath may take thirty seconds to completely fill the lungs and twenty seconds to empty them. The slower the intake, the more fully the lungs are able to expand.

Practice:

Try this now. Relax your breathing to slow, calm breaths. Open your nostrils and notice how air automatically pours in. Close your nostrils and notice the difficulty you have trying to breathe in. The air flows according to how open your nostrils are.

Now don't try to breath, focus instead on just opening your chest by using your muscle to expand the chest. Try not to draw air in. Instead, allow air in as your chest expands and your lungs make room for air and fill up automatically. Do this slowly, gently. Now simultaneously open your nostrils while you open your chest. Do this in a relaxed fashion. If any muscles tense up, start again. Everything should be relaxed and calm. If you can do this exercise for several minutes, your body will automatically take over and you will fill with so much oxygen that you will wonder how you ever survived without this much air before.

Life flows according to how open you are. When you are closed to flow you are in resistance.

I exhale slowly by using my chest muscle to squeeze the air out of my lungs. In order to get my body to take over and do this automatically, first I pause at the top and bottom of each breath. After several minutes, I consciously don't take the next breath. Then I wait for my body to do it naturally, without my focus. If I have been doing the breathing smoothly for several minutes, with little thought, then the body knows how I want to breathe and it takes over without my conscious effort. When this happens my breathing feels completely effortless, far more than ever before. Within a minute or a few minutes, it feels like my skin begins to breathe while oxygen pours into every inch of my body. I feel light and rich with oxygen with invincible health, saturated with life. It sounds amazing, and it really is. It took me several tries to really master this breathing. When I have not done it for a while, then I have to spend time practicing again.

One of the powerful benefits of this breathing technique comes into play when I am in a stressful situation, be it traffic, a disgruntled person, or physical pain. I turn to this method while I am sitting or walking and I am immediately calmed in a way that the stress does not affect me. It works like an instant chill pill, and a pain reliever. This breathing trains the body to breathe deeper and receive oxygen for total body wellness. It is a natural way to instantly relieve tension.

To further enhance my experience, I place my focus on my body. I start with my feet. I notice and feel the soles, toes, tops, and heels. The more details I notice, the more relaxed I feel as my mind clears to allow for this awareness. It works well to further clear my mind of random thoughts. Next I include my ankles, adding them to the awareness to my feet. I add my calf muscles, my shins and the skin around my lower legs. I include all parts of my knees, my hamstrings, and quadriceps and my thighs including bones and blood. While doing this I am still conscious of all the body areas I have already visited, and am aware that my breathing stays relaxed.

I move my awareness to my pelvis and include my female organs, hip bones and buttocks. Next I include my kidneys, spleen, liver, stomach, diaphragm, lower lung, upper lung and heart. Then I add in my spine. All the while I stop occasionally to be sure that my awareness also remains with the body parts that I have included so far. I picture a white light moving to each area and warming it.

When I reach my upper chest, I pause and include both hands, palms, fingers, then lower arms, elbows, upper arms and shoulders. I focus on my neck, scalp, skull, eyes, tongue, the roof of my mouth, teeth, ears, eye sockets and brain. At this point my body feels light, energized and flowing with energy. I relax and enjoy the physical pleasure while my body releases pain and stress, feeling rejuvenated. So often you lose awareness of your body as your mind drifts from one demand to another. Bringing the focus back to the body feels great and sends powerful energy into your physical form.

If you find it difficult to feel each body area, you can wiggle each part as you bring your awareness to it. Or have a partner help you by touching each area as you relax and focus your awareness into your body. With practice this becomes much easier.

I found The Reconnection was the key for me in learning to meditate. The Reconnection brought me to the meditative state so that I knew what I was shooting for when I laid down to do it. There are many audio tapes available as well. The practice of mind relaxation has tremendous health benefits as well as the benefit to helping you live and create in the zone.

Once you learn how to bring your awareness into your body, you can use a faster technique to meditate with the same results. I picture meridian lines in my body running from my big toes, up my legs and past my hips. I feel this energy move while I picture it. The meridian lines run along both sides of my torso toward my neck. Simultaneously, two meridian lines run up my arms, beginning at my index finger and meeting at my neck. Those lines meet with the other two meridian lines from my legs. The four lines travel up my neck, into my head, and meet at my third eye chakra (energy center between my eye brows) to become one meridian line, which then travels out of my head, through my crown chakra (energy center on the top of my head) and meets with all of the energy in the universe. This exercise puts my spirit and consciousness totally into my body, connecting body, mind and spirit. From this amazing space I have healed my body of many ailments, rejuvenated my energy, balanced my chakras and felt deep peace.

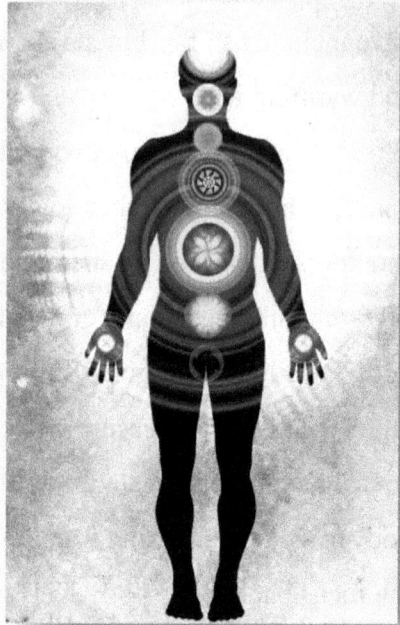

These powerful meditations bring in energy, so I can heal myself from headaches, neck aches, and almost any kind of pain within twenty minutes. I no longer have frequent neck pain. About eight months after I learned how to do this, I decided to meditate to help some severe neck pain that was with me daily for the previous twenty-five years. During the meditation I directed large amounts of white light to my neck, and then pictured this energy filling, warming, relaxing and healing my neck. After twenty minutes, my neck adjusted itself while I was lying in meditation. I felt and heard a bone move into place, with instant and lasting relief. Twenty-five years of neck pain healed in one meditation.

In addition to having the ability to heal your own body, you also are gifted with the ability to ground the energy around you. You will begin to feel this power as you become more grounded yourself. We all need the energy of the earth to enjoy optimal well-being. Tune your awareness into the rustic ambiance of nature and the needs of the planet. Walk barefoot on the grass or sand while you acknowledge the earth below your feet. Observe birds, the moon, sun and stars. Care for plants and animals. Connect deeply with a pet, or a person you love, or our planet. Imagine that you're connected to the earth with roots like a tree that sprout from your feet. Your roots reach deep into the ground where you feel the cool touch of the moist soil while you receive the healing nourishment that you need. Imagine all of your pain and emotional charge releasing into the earth as she receives your old programs and transforms them into nutrients.

Once you are grounded and in the zone, you can tap into your personal vibrations instead of the patterns around you. Patterns are like computer programs. They run until you tell them to stop, turn them off, or you rewrite the program. Meditation and breathing allow you to reset the operating systems, so new instructions can occur.

Before I change the energy in a home office or building, I bring myself into the zone with a fast meditation technique. Through regular practice with meditation, I have trained myself to ground my awareness in the physical body quickly when needed. I sit on the floor, close my eyes and focus on my heart. I breathe calmly and bring my awareness into my entire body. I clear my mind, letting go of all attachments and thoughts. I enter a place of just awareness, connected to all consciousness, the space around me and with the earth. Because I have been here often, I know how to find this place quickly. At this point, I am ready to proceed to the next step in the process.

In this heightened state of awareness, you can connect with your creative power. When you are in the zone, effort, doubt and fear do not exist. Enter this place understanding that you now have command of the energy around you.

4 Owning Your Power

Everything we desire is already within us: Love, happiness, peace and abundance. Harnessing these powers means we sow the seeds for real change. ~Edwin Mamerto

Sending You Love

As I write this, I silently go within my being and radiate love out to you, the reader. My heart is full as I feel you. I am grateful for you, my fellow human who has chosen to experience earth with me at this time. I am grateful for who you are, your energy and how you have chosen to shine your light.

You are Light

Science and intuition has allowed us to understand that everything we see and don't see is comprised of light.[11] Dr. Jill Bolte Taylor is a neuroscientist who had a massive stroke at age thirty seven. She wrote a book about her experience titled, *My Stroke of Insight*. In the book she explains that her left hemisphere shut down due to massive bleeding. She only had access to her right hemisphere. Through this experience she teaches us that our right hemisphere is responsible for our

---

[11] Shows the light spectrum. The visible spectrum is a faction of the whole.
http://imagine.gsfc.nasa.gov/docs/science/know_l1/emspectrum.html

intuition, feelings, emotions, inner knowing, insight, imagination and connection with nature and people, as well as being present without the ego. It is the creative side of our brain and how we feel and sense the world around us. To use this book you will need to invite your right hemisphere to participate. Your left brain is responsible for language and reading this material. Your left brain will have to become quiet for you to connect to the land, or a house, and to sense the energy around you. Jill became very good at this when the left side of her brain was "off-line."[12]

Take a moment to go within and feel the light that is you. Say to yourself, "I am light." Be sure that you understand this about yourself.

You and I are the same. You are a powerful soul, or piece of God, sharing your interpretation of the world and shining that understanding back out toward others. You might say to yourself, "I could never be a CEO. I was not born with enough brains. I could never dance. I have two left feet. I couldn't write a book: I can't sit that long." Your self-talk is your interpretation of what is. It doesn't mean that it is actually true. Although, if you believe your self-talk, then it is true for you. Your self-talk sets your limits.

---

[12] http://drjilltaylor.com/

The Power of Decision

Please take out a blank piece of paper. At the top write the words, "I decide." Do you know how powerful the words "I decide" are? Think about it. I decided to get married. I decided to move to Texas. I decided to love my brother unconditionally. I decided to have a baby. I decided to start a business. Decisions change your life. Resolves move you forward in a certain direction. If you are on a trail with two paths you must make a decision in order to move forward. If you don't decide, then you are standing still. Make your choices, and make them wisely.

You are made of pure light. That light radiates out from you to the world around you. You decide how that light shines forth. Think of people that you know. If there is someone in the room with you right now observe them. Notice the light others are putting forth. Can you see how they are shining their light? Are they doing it consciously or is their light just leaking out from an unconscious place?

What about you? What light are you radiating outwardly? Are you doing it consciously? Are you projecting the radiance that you want others to see? Have you made a decision about what luminosity you want to share with the world? It is your choice how you shine.

On your piece of paper, after the words "I Decide," write "How I will Shine My Light." I would like for you to get quiet. Spend several minutes deciding how you will project yourself.

Are there areas of your life right now where you are compromising your brightness for another person? You don't need to compromise your energy. If others are taking your energy, then you are not radiating forth the real you.

You could decide to shine the glow of a tough cowboy, who is strong, good with animals, protective and honorable. Perhaps you're a mother who wants to shine by example, teach and nurture, help other mothers and be a helpful neighbor. Maybe you are a counselor who will decide to teach others how to make good choices for themselves to promote self-healing. Perhaps you're a grandfather and your brightness is love for your grandkids.

Whatever you decide, it is important to be clear that you are being who you wish the world to see. Your brilliance is your gift to others. Are you representing yourself the way you want? Are you being true to your essence?

Never Compromise You

If you are not being true or you feel down and unhappy, then there is a simple way to take the steps toward projecting your true inner glow. After you write "I Decide How I will Shine My Light," write the following statement: "I will not compromise my energy." What this means is that you will discontinue making choices that do not lift your energy. You will stop doing things, saying things and thinking things that bring your energy down. I am not talking about giving help when you don't feel like it or avoiding social opportunities because you're not in the mood. Those things are good for you. That's like not eating your vegetables because you would rather have chocolate or beer. You should do the things that are good for you, even when you don't feel like it. Chances are that if you don't want to help others then you have closed down your heart. When your heart is open again, you will enjoy helping others and attending social events.

Not compromising your energy means avoiding everything that is not honest. It means avoiding relationships, people and situations that do not have integrity. It means not agreeing to do things that bring you down or are not true to your essence. You will learn with practice what staying true to yourself feels like. You will notice that it feels energizing.

Examples of not being true would be: becoming a doctor because your parents wanted you to be one when you wanted to be a stand-up comedian, or getting married to your lover because you were afraid of being alone, or you didn't get divorced because you didn't want to let your parents down. When you compromise, you hurt yourself. Inside you know what feels good and what does not. If you are ashamed to tell others what you are doing or have done, then you probably compromised yourself. Don't beat yourself up or judge yourself, just stop doing it from today forward.

Start by making a list of any and all ways that you could improve your integrity to yourself, your purpose and your essence. Then make a list of the ways that you will begin today to change the ways that you are out of integrity with yourself. List what you will do differently. This is a very important step to write down. Do not leave this in your head. This list will catapult you into your power.

It will be difficult for you to have a powerful centered energy to influence everything around you when you are out of integrity with your true-self. As you align your actions with who you are, you will feel a boost in strength. That boost will enable your powerful self to change your world.

Letting Go of Draining Emotions

There is one more thing that will help you gather your energy so that you will be in your full power when you begin to direct the light around you. Your emotional state needs to be one of power, not weakness. The emotions of anger, guilt, shame, embarrassment, jealousy, hurt and sadness all weaken your energy force. These emotions steal precious life-force from you. It is helpful for you to see that these emotions do not serve you, but instead rob you of vitality.

Take anger for example. It is possible to drive beside a distracted, rude driver without becoming angry. It is possible to discipline a small child without anger. You can wait in a long line without feeling anger. You can watch the news and even participate in a community organized standoff with government without displaying and feeling anger. You can be productive in

48

all ways without the influence of anger. Anger takes your energy. In order to balance your energy and the energy around you, you must be in a state that empowers you.

Feelings such as love, peace, joy, empathy, kindness, caring, generosity, gratitude, forgiveness, understanding and compassion strengthen your power. Entering these states is as easy as aligning with your integrity and then deciding to open your heart. Once you are in integrity with your heart open, these emotional states will be present for you. How you feel is a choice. You get to decide, every day.

There will be times that come up to test your emotional resilience. When we have not dealt with past emotions, new experiences come up again and again until we face experiences in a healthy, mature way. If you have neglected to deal with anger at your father, new experiences will anger you until you completely feel and release the emotion. Realize that you have the option available to you at all times to let emotions move through you and then choose a new emotional state. You can chose to feel angry, or you can admit why the situation is not aligned with who you are and then you can choose how you will respond, without allowing draining emotions to control you or your behavior.

Know that You are Powerful

Influencing your world is something that you do every single day. The second that you have an expectation, you influence your experience. Each thought that slips across your consciousness or unconsciousness influences what is happening around you. You may not be able to control every second of your experience with conscious thought, but we can't say for sure that somehow you are not creating every part of your experience.

On a quantum level we can see how this works. Einstein noticed this effect when he did the famous Double-Slit Experiment. Einstein was initially confused, then he noticed that particles acted differently when they were observed than they did when they were not observed. When a light particle was shot out of a photon gun at a wall with two slits on it, sometimes the photon would go through one slit and other times it would pass through both slits simultaneously. When it passed through one slit, Einstein said that the photon acted like a particle. When it went through both slits at the same time, he said the photon acted like a wave. The interesting point is that the photons acted like particles, passing through one slit, when no one was looking. If there was an observer, then the photon passed through both slits, acting like a wave.

It took Einstein a bit of testing to figure this out. Essentially he concluded that your observation changes the photons around you. Your observation and expectations influence how the photons behave. Mothers see this in real time when they notice that a three year old might behave differently while being watched versus when the three year old is alone. Cats and dogs are good examples as well. Children and pets often act according to our expectations and observations. Most of life is the same.

Law of Attraction

Embrace the unexpected as if you wished for it all along.

Not only do we influence what happens, but we also interpret it. Two people might see the same car accident and yet they may not agree on what happened and they definitely won't use the same words to describe what happened. When emotions, voice tones and facial expressions are involved, there are many ways that people will interpret the same situation. Your beliefs influence how you see the world. <u>Sometimes all you need to change your experience is to change your beliefs.</u> If this information is challenging for you to accept, all you have to do is change your belief and suddenly your heart tells you that you really are powerful enough to influence the energy around you.

I have a close friend who has traveled the world by herself. She has been to India, Peru, Thailand, Singapore, Costa

Rica and many other countries without a tour guide or male escort. When people mention that it is dangerous to travel alone, she always responds the same, "It's not dangerous if you feel like you belong there. Act like you know what you are doing and no one will bother you. I expect people to be helpful to me and that is what I always experience." I traveled to Costa Rica with her. We had a very safe and pleasant experience, while other people who stayed in our hotel were robbed of everything they brought: money, passports, and credit cards. They were not surprised. We were shocked. We experienced people being helpful to us, even young men carrying our bags.

You have heard the expression, "You get out of life exactly what you expect." It is true. You are creating your experience with your expectation. The golden secret is to intentionally choose which of your expectations are creating your world. That means choosing your thoughts wisely, expecting to get what you want. What is difficult to accept is that you receive what you focus on. It's amazing how this works. And it works to your detriment too. If you focus on how little money you have, you will have more challenges with having very little money. If you focus on your belly fat, you will continue to have belly fat. The opposite is true as well. If you focus on how flat your stomach is, you will experience more of the same. If you focus on your good complexion, your skin will improve. If you focus on how sick you feel, you will feel worse. You attract to you what you feel on a regular basis.

The best way to begin to influence your world is to determine exactly what you would like to influence right now. Be very clear. If you want a house close to bike trails so you will exercise outdoor every day, don't focus on having a million dollars to buy a big house in the hills. Feel as if you already have the trails right by your house. Feel how happy you are that the trails are easy for you to access and how great you feel going for a ride each day out your front door. Remember, you will get the same thing that you are focused on, so focus on what you want to create. Don't give energy to what you don't want or focus on just the money. The emotion is the power that brings your dreams forward.

At Your Disposal

Now that you know how powerful you are to influence your world, know that there is energy all around you that is at your command. There is no such thing as empty space. It does not exist. Scientists have proven it. The air around you is full of energy, although you can't see it. The air is filled with light that is not in our spectrum of vision. These light particles are ready, willing and able to be influenced by your thoughts, intentions and beliefs. Your best opportunity to direct this energy is to be fully present.

If someone would have told me to become fully present six years ago, I wouldn't have known how to do it. I was lucky. A friend asked me if I wanted to be reconnected. I trusted her, so I said yes. I couldn't meditate or become deeply present before I was Reconnected through the process called The Reconnection, taught by Dr. Eric Pearl.[13] This technique brought me to a place where I merged my energy with all energy. I felt one with all. It was the most blissful, ecstatic feeling I have ever had. Afterwards, I knew how to become present. It took practice, but I could do it.

If you are reading this book you may already know how to become fully present. Being full conscious means that you can feel your body and you are aware of the moment. You are not thinking about the future or the past. Ego is not controlling you when you and your influence or your experience is much more powerful. I have meditated fully cognizant and healed my neck. Twenty-five years of pain disappeared in an instant. When you are present you smell the air, flowers, pine trees, hear birds and feel very differently than you do when you are in your head and not present.

This book is not enough to teach you how to become present if you don't know how. But I am here to tell you of the power you hold at your disposal when you enter this state. You can practice with it in the grocery store, with your neighbor or

---

[13] http://www.thereconnection.com/

family. Speak to someone when you are fully present, self-aware and aware of everything going on around you. If your ego is completely gone and you are only in the moment, your influence is far reaching.

Know Your Worth

It is difficult to step into your power when you are beating yourself up. Maybe you compare your looks to others, or your salary, or your house. Perhaps you beat on yourself for not getting married, for not doing more volunteer work, or for not being a better parent. No matter how you put yourself down, self-attacks and difficult measuring sticks are slowing you down. Every human has made serious errors. We all deserve a break and self-forgiveness. On the contrary, when you realize how powerful you are, you give yourself permission to use your abilities.

Deep inside you know that a person's worth is not based on appearances, money or intelligence. Yes, society values these things. But take an infant as an example. A new born child does not have wealth, looks or wisdom. Yet humans always put a high worth on an infant. The bottom line is that being born gives you worth. Being alive makes you valuable. A conscious brain gives you power. Being an observer makes you a creator. You are a valuable, powerful creator. Own these traits and you increase your control over your experience.

You can increase your feeling of worth by listing human characteristics that you admire and will emulate. These might include generosity, kindness, empathy, compassion, honesty, self-conviction, affection, being true to oneself. Once you decide which traits you will incorporate into your actions, you will feel good about your contribution as a powerful creator.

Another way to increase your value and worth is to decide what you will create that benefits others, as well as yourself. When you are setting your goals, you might decide you want a nice home, new skis, a travel budget and a soul mate. These are the things you want to create for yourself. Since you are so powerful, find something that you are passionate about for others. Would you like to find housing for the homeless, volunteer to give food to the hungry or would you like to volunteer for a Planning and Zoning Commission? What are you passionate about that you can give to the world? How can you use your creative powers to make the world a better habitat?

Take time now and write how you will use your creative power to experience what you want. Then write how you will create a better experience for others. Use the space below.

- Your Personal Goals:

- Your Goals to Contribute to the World:

5 Communicating with All:

Earth is sentient and aware. Her awareness affects humanity.

By reciprocity, the reverse is also true.

Those who dwell among the beauties and mysteries of the earth

are never alone or weary of life. ~Rachel Carson

After I reconnected the home of an acquaintance, I received this note from her.

Diana,
This evening, I took a minute to sit quietly and ask my house if he was feeling better and more appreciated now after being reconnected. Almost immediately, I got this vivid sensation of glowing, reddish-gold, humming warmth spreading from my feet through my whole body. It wasn't just a vague impression, it was all-enveloping. At the same time, a BIG smile spread across my face that did not feel at all like my own smile.

It was as if he answered by inhabiting my body for a few moments to let me feel how great he feels instead of trying to tell me about it. Then he gently left me and went back to being a house.

It rocked. I loved it.
Peggy

As my personal relationship with the earth grew, I became aware of the importance of respect for the land we inhabit and develop. I learned that our thoughts and feelings toward the land, and everything around us, reflect our internal relationship.

I learned to offer gratitude for the trees used to build my home, the sand used to make my windows and the gravel used to fortify my foundation. As I developed this appreciation, and expressed it, my relationship with my home became one of gratitude and respect. My reverence for all of creation, for its essence and contribution in my life, kept my ego in check once I acknowledged the forces of nature and the resources of earth.

As I cultivated this admiration, a shift occurred within my being. I could connect with every creation. I could now feel the spirit of the land and connect my energy with it when I was in the zone. As I connected, I expressed an affectionate apology for any disrespect and mistreatment the land received in the past from anyone. I asked the land for permission to connect it to any structures occupying it. Each time I have done this, I always feel the land's appreciation in return.

After reconnection, I discovered how to communicate with the land through my feelings and thoughts. I don't use a formula. I communicate from my heart what I feel in the moment. Every situation feels different. I express love and respect, and then I ask the energy of the land and environment if I may proceed with the connection. I can now accomplish this with simple focus, but in the beginning it was easier for me if I walked on the land, or sat quietly on the land for a little while, or touched the soil and plants. I physically connect through touch first, and then I connect internally also. This simple process works with practice. Practice by walking around noticing how things make you feel. Then convert your experience into words. Home decorators, architects, real estate agents and Feng Shui practitioners can articulate how they feel in a home, building or on a piece of land. With a little practice, you can as well.

Tuning into a space grounds me to the land and structure and releases my judgments about the property. Then I can open up the patterns in the home to all possibilities, without feeling attached to the outcome. If I focus on a certain result, my expectations limit the possible outcomes. Having no expectation allows you more healing and broader possibilities.

I check in to see if I feel good about proceeding. I usually receive a feeling of peace, excitement and gratitude. If I come across a situation where I don't feel comfortable with proceeding, then I would know that I do not have permission. This process of connecting my energy and obtaining permission takes me about two to four minutes. Allow for the amount of time that you need without rushing.

Permission from a home appears more complex and less straight forward than the land. Each connection feels similar in some ways, yet unique. Frequently I feel the energy of the home ask me how connecting will benefit it. I speak with the home in my mind as directly as possible.

Talking with the home, I sense its vibrations and describe what I feel, much like our brain converts sound waves into words. I simply notice what I feel and trust it. I receive requests from homes such as, "I want to feel appreciated," or "I want to feel connected with the family who lives here." I sense empty homes feel lonely and want people to fill them with laughter so they fulfill their purpose. If the home makes a request, I simply program the grid to include the request.

Connecting with a home has a similar effect as connecting with a person or animal. Afterwards you feel that you established a relationship, a knowing of them and their personality; such as when we connected with our car or a favorite chair. I notice any place in the home that draws my attention and how it feels to place my awareness on that space. I focus on sensations in my body, such as impressions, thoughts and feelings.

I build a grid and spiral to create the energy pattern of the fingerprint of all creation, fractal geometry and the Golden mean.

Once the home is grounded, the shift in energy might be minor at first. It may take days or weeks for it to noticeably improve, and it may need to be balanced more than once. But if I feel an improvement in the energy, then I know that I have strengthened the field and brought in natural frequencies.

Every building is an entity with its own unique essence; therefore I find great variety in the energy in buildings, much like the variety in the personalities of people and animals. Imagine that you were given the task to describe the traits of several homes. You would find several words to explain the look, feel and atmosphere of each property. We might use words like bold, soft, friendly, welcoming, complicated, busy, tense, relaxing, soothing, irritating or quiet. Many of the same words we use to describe people describe buildings. Homes radiate a kind of *personality* about them.

My close friend Dawn asked me to connect one of her investment homes because it was listed on the market but was not receiving any interest during the poor housing market. I met Dawn at the house to do the connection process.

As I entered this home, I noticed that I felt heavy and out of balance. This feeling continued as I walked through the home. The home was also imbalanced architecturally. On one side of the entry was a single story living area with three exterior walls. On the other side of the entry was the rest of the three thousand square foot, two-story home. The pattern of this home was far different than what is natural to us, or to creations.

I took the time to get very quiet and pay attention to all of the many feelings I experienced in the home. I felt drawn to sit down on the dining room floor. I expanded my own energy field so that it touched everything around me. I imagined my field stretching out to include the land, animal life, plants and insects. The land below Dawn's house was "ready" and I felt comfortable with proceeding.

I sat quietly, placed my awareness throughout the home and noticed how it felt. I didn't judge it or try to fix it. I discerned how the home would feel if its essence were appreciated for the amazing creation that it was. I did all of this with my heart while being fully present, leaving my ego out of it. I asked if I could connect the home to the earth and the universe with a magnetic field. Although Dawn's home was excited to hear from me and thrilled about being connected, which I could tell by the excitement that I felt about proceeding, I felt a lot of negativity hanging around, as if someone disliked the home, and that emotion hung in the air. The home wanted to feel better.

"Dawn, I feel many heavy, negative words hanging in the air here; thoughts such as 'this home falls short.' This home has a feeling like a teenage girl with low self-esteem, because she heard someone say over and over that she was not good enough. Do you know what this is all about?"

"Actually you just picked up my energy by mistake. Those were my teenage years," Dawn joked.

"It's funny you should say that Dawn. Homes often feel similar to their owner. A loving person has a very welcoming vibration in their home. A grumpy person's home has an unwelcoming vibration present. But I know you and it's not coming from you. So why do you think this home feels inferior?"

"Well, this home was used as a real estate sales office for a period of time. When the sales agents met with clients in this home, they were selling other homes and talking about how wonderful the other homes were in the neighborhood. Most of the agents didn't really like this home. So that makes sense."

"We need to take the negative words out. Words are energy that can linger. Connecting the home brings in natural frequencies to make the home feel more comfortable, but we can also remove the vibration of the old words that remain. We should probably smudge[14] this home, although I didn't bring any sage. Since I didn't bring sage, we can use our determination to send the words away and replace them with positive statements about the house."

"Do you think intention will do it?" she asked.

"Absolutely, belief in our own power will suffice. Rituals express our aspirations, but we're the power behind it. Our voice is an excellent tool for projecting our intention."

"Okay, I believe that," Dawn said convinced.

"We want to shift the vibration of this home to feel attractive, with beautiful finishes, a functional floor plan and worthy to a loving family."

---

[14] Ancient tradition of burning sage to wipe-out old vibrations and clear the energy. Often used by Native Americans.

"Great. Let's do it."

"Let me just see if I missed anything." I then proceeded to connect more with the home to feel for other needs. As I connected my emotional energy with the home, I also felt a deep sense of longing for people to love the home.

"Now I feel the energy of loneliness. This house feels deserted." I said.

"Well, this was a busy place for a while. Now it has been empty for many months. The space felt more active and alive when we were here every day. Since we pulled out, maybe it feels abandoned. But don't all vacant homes feel that way?"

"I suppose they do, but the energy in this home feels gloomy. The house misses having people here every day. It wants to fulfill its purpose as a home for a family. It has a sad feeling due to emptiness."

"Well, what can we do?" Dawn asked as if she didn't expect any solution.

"I am not sure." I stopped to reflect and see what came to me. "We could try something." I paused and she gave me a curious look. "We could try imagining that a family lives here. Imagination works wonders. Our imagination can place a family here who loves this home so it won't feel so lonely." I paused again, looking at her with my 'what do you think?' expression. "Do you want to try it?" I asked.

"Why not?" she said, clearly not convinced that imagination would suffice.

"Our imagination is very powerful, especially when we involve the body in the imagining. How would your body feel if a family lived here? How would this home feel different?"

Dawn and I walked around clearing the negative words away by imagining that we could gather them and send them out the door. We paid compliments to the house, leaving our positive words in the home. "What a beautiful fireplace. I love this large, multi-purpose, bonus room. Look at these gorgeous cabinets. Some family yearns to live here."

Then we each imagined that a family moved in, lived in the home and loved it.

"This house needs a name, so we feel more connected to it."

"Okay," Dawn said. "What name do you think?"

"She feels like a Brianna to me."

"Get out!" Dawn shouted. "That exact name popped into my head as soon as you said that she needed a name."

We continued the connection process. I programmed into the grid for it to find a happy family to appreciate it, and feel welcomed. It took one month for Brianna to sell to a wonderful family.

A few weeks later Dawn called me. "Brianna has a wonderful family occupying her with a Lease-Purchase

Agreement in place. Thank you for helping me fix her. I wish you could fix my romantic relationships as fast."

It's been almost five years since I connected Brianna and the same family still lives there.

"Dawn, we didn't exactly fix Brianna. We loved her from our higher consciousness and allowed her pattern to change."

"Whatever. She feels fixed."

"Now if we could only fix you," I said teasingly with a huge smile.

"Thanks a lot!" she said pretending to be offended. "Hey, wouldn't it be nice to have a friendship with a house or car the way we can with people? It would be cool if we could be friends with a favorite tree we sit under."

"Dawn, it is possible. Everything you see is made out of the same energy. Yes, we have a brain and heart, but all energy has consciousness from the source of all energy. So we can communicate with all of it. Many people say that they feel the conscious energy of plants. Studies have been done on the connections between people and plants. Some experiments have shown that plants respond to our thoughts. Some people can connect with rocks as well, like grounding and connection with the earth."

"Then I am going to communicate to the squirrels to stop eating the center of my tulips and the birds to layoff my strawberries."

"That will work as well as asking your six-year old to stop eating candy. But you could communicate your love and appreciation for the wildlife and ask them to stay in harmony with your garden. The messages that we give out come back to us. Your words are powerful and they do make an impact."

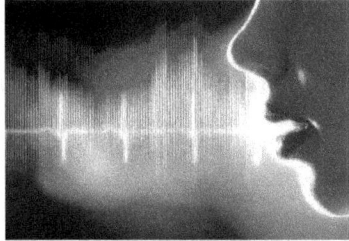

Let's review.

How to influence the vibrations around you:

1. Visualize with clarity how you want to feel.

☐   Example: I love where I live and work (now feel it).

2. Imagine that you experience the feeling along with gratitude.

☐   Example: I feel gratitude for my home. I am blessed to live in a place I enjoy so tremendously (now feel it).

3. Choose words and actions which support that you already feel the way you want to.

☐   Example: I take very good care of my home and share its pleasant atmosphere with loved ones (now feel it).

4. Program your environment to support your desired vibrations.

☐   Example: I program this home to emit the vibrations of love, happiness and gratitude so that I feel love and peace in my home (now feel it).

5.   Maintain the focus on how you want to feel.

☐   Example: I trust the universe/God to lead me to where I am happy. My heart feels content wherever I live. Unlimited options abound (now feel it).

6 A Bridge Between Light and Matter

Ere many Generations pass, our machinery will be driven by a power obtained at any point in the universe. ~Nicola Tesla

It followed from the special theory of relativity that mass and energy are both but different manifestations of the same thing — a somewhat unfamiliar conception for the average mind. ~Albert Einstein

Tesla taught that the air and earth are full of vast energy that is enough to power all that man invents without the need for turbines, coal and petroleum. This free energy is accessible to everyone who knows how to tap into it. [15]

Not everyone understands the energy available in our dimension. Only a few realize the powerful resources all around us. Tesla gave us the radio, alternating electric current, remote

---

[15] Explains Tesla's theory of free energy
http://www.greenstone.org/greenstone3/nzdl?a=d&d=HASH0 107648ee466d1b75f493474.21&c=cdl&sib=1&dt=&ec=&et=& p.a=b&p.s=ClassifierBrowse&p.sa=   *"Natures Amplifier"*, **Science 83**, July, August, 1983, pg. 7.

control and hydropower. He understood the power available in the universe, explaining that unlimited energy exists everywhere.

> Throughout space there is energy, it is a
> mere question of time when men will
> succeed in attaching their machinery to the
> very wheelwork of Nature....The
> knowledge that there is, throbbing through
> the Earth, energy available everywhere,
> would exert a strong stimulus on students,
> mechanics and inventors of all countries.
> This would be productive of infinite good.
> Conditions such as never existed before
> would be brought about. It would enable
> man to dispense with the necessity of
> mining, pumping, transporting and burning
> of fuels, and so do away with innumerable
> causes of waste! New frontiers might be
> opened, unlimited power for all the world,
> inexpensive power for the farmer to light
> and heat his home, to drive his tractor, to
> harvest his grain, to increase his food
> output, electric power for millions of
> homes, so economical that every appliance
> could be operated electrically. Tesla

I experience the unlimited energy available each time I connect with it to balance the energy in a building. When I connect myself with this power, to construct a virtual energy grid, I use my power as creator, combined with heart-felt love. I am in the zone, able to change energy. In the process, I experience a peaceful renewal of my own energy that motivates me to continue to use this dynamic ability.

When I change the energy, buildings do not appear differently to the eyes, yet they feel different. Of the complete light wave spectrum of energy around us, the human eye only sees a tiny percentage of the total band. We cannot see the infrared rays, ultra-violet, x-rays, gamma, microwave, heat waves and radio waves. Yet they often impact physical matter: microwaves cook food, radio waves give us sound.

The energy in buildings impacts our quality of life. We feel the impact, similarly to the way we can feel the love or hate in the atmosphere between two people. We can often feel anger in a room, but we can't see it.

If a home or office is not providing an optimal environment, then it is in your best interest to improve the space for your health and well-being. The best way to improve the energy in buildings is to allow in lots of direct and indirect sunlight, plenty of fresh air, incorporate plants indoors, make sure every appliance is grounded, use extra grounding techniques and rid the space of annoying appliance vibrations and replace with pleasant music, indoor waterfalls, or sounds of nature. When these options are not available, or if they are not enough, then you must resort to connecting the building through intention and being completely present with the energy. I find the simplest and most effective way to focus in on a building is by setting up a new grid.

The systems in the human body, as well as all visible matter, intricately connect in patterns we label as a grid. Einstein talked

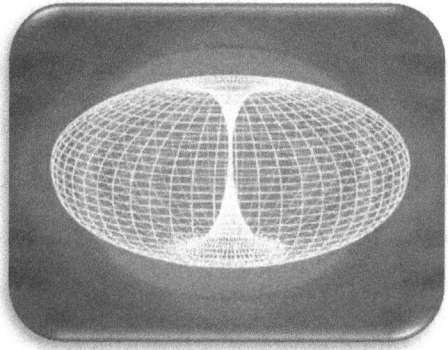

about the grid that he called the *fabric of the universe*.

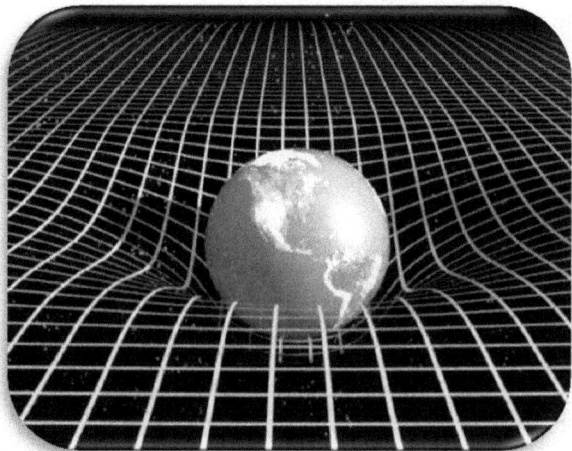

We see this fabric reflected in our physical world everywhere; the eyes of a fly, the skin of a lizard, the shell of a turtle.

Magnetic fields form grid-like patterns similar to the ones we see in nature, to hold the pattern of the mass in place so it will stay the same and not defuse back into unorganized energy. Humans use many kinds of grids as well. The internet, radar, longitude and latitude, sonar, mapping, scanning, x-rays and our own body's magnetic fields all follow the patterning of grids. Our body's skeletal system, endocrine system, nervous system, lymph system, vascular system, pulmonary system all comprise intricate networks functioning together like a grid. Like the energy field of an atom or person, grids connect things and keep the vibrational pattern in tack.

When we connect a building's energy field, we can include the pattern we desire for that space. The grid will hold the patterns.

The Process of Connecting a Building

1. I first ground myself through a meditation such as one of the methods discussed earlier.

2. From my place of center, without ego, I connect my energy with the land and home while noticing the feelings.

3. I ask the land, then the building, for permission to connect the structure. I pause until I receive an inner feeling of peace. When the peace comes, my body naturally sighs. Internally I feel excited to proceed. I take the next step, to build the grid which I will cover in full details a little later.

Recently I connected a friend's home. Tina owns a newer home with many of the popular features of today. I observed the home from the outside, noticed the shape, to determine what geometric shape grid I should create to surround it. Ideally I use a square cube, but it does not always work for all buildings. Tina's home was rectangular in shape, so I chose that shape for my grid. I visualized a three dimensional rectangular cube around her home, enclosing the entire building equidistant above and below the surface.

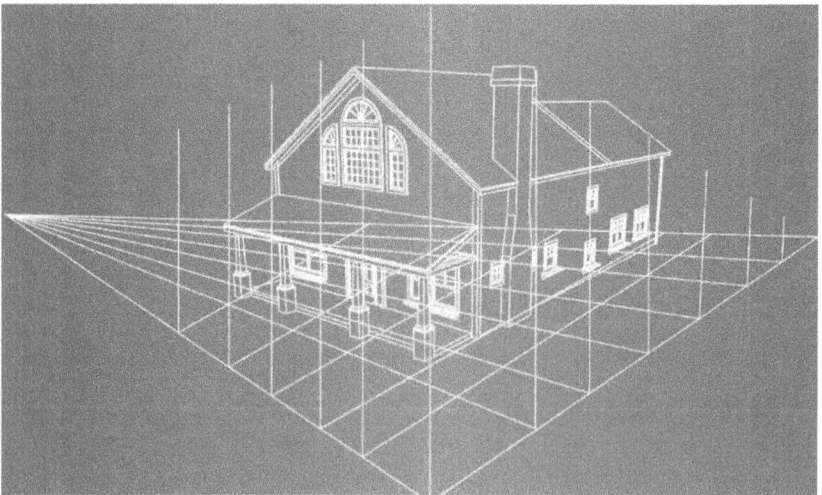

Here is a quick overview of the next steps to connecting Tina's home:

1. I needed to place a virtual pillar at each corner of the rectangle. Beginning at her front door, going clockwise, I walked to the location of the first pillar, the corner point of the rectangle. I visually lined up the location with the corner edge of her roof line, carefully making certain to include all of her home. When you connect a building, always include the entire structure, being careful not to leave any part of the home outside of the grid. If one area of the house protrudes beyond the corner point, then I locate the pillar away from the corner of the house to enclose the protruding point.

2. Standing directly behind the pillar site, I stretched my arms out to make a circle around the virtual pillar. My arms could rest at my sides, but outstretched arms around the pillar help me visualize the pillar's location. While centered, I created an invisible pillar made of energy, with my imagination. At Tina's home I saw in my imagination, and felt with my body, the pillar grow from below the surface, deep in the soil, up though my arms to the height of the highest point on the roof or chimney. The pillar is equal length above ground as well as below ground.

3. I stated in my mind, "I create this pillar of equal depth from below the surface up to the height to the highest point on this home. My words create my intention. I could do this silently

speaking in my head. Then I felt a small, subtle rush of energy in front of me as the pillar grew, like a soft breeze that I felt on the inside of my body rather than the outside. When the first pillar was completed, my body automatically took a deep breath, followed by a sigh. The experience may feel different for you, but a spontaneous sigh represents a good sign of completion for me.

4. I walked around the home clockwise stopping at each corner to repeat the process, creating the pillar with intention, visualizing it, waiting for the sigh, until I had created all four pillars of the rectangle.

I made my pillars large enough in diameter to support a grid around Tina's home based on the overall size. When you do this exercise, create a size that feels right to you or ask yourself intuitively to make the pillar the correct diameter to create a stable grid. Creating each pillar takes me between five to twenty seconds. If I get distracted, or when I do not feel as confident, it takes me longer.

Note: if you want to connect a structure from a distance, such as a building in another location or country, do all of the work in your mind, picturing the location of each pillar. You still need permission of the land, environment and structure. Distance does not exist in energy work. It isn't relative.

5. Next I needed to connect the pillars to each other with cables of light to give strength to the grid. I located myself in the

middle of her home, or as close to the true middle as I could determine. When I could not stand in the middle, then in my mind I located myself in the center. From the middle of her home, with my imagination, I strung a clear, two inch cable of light from the top of pillar one to the bottom of pillar three. I used my right arm with my index finger pointing to the pillar. Drawing a line in the air, I visualized the cable of light as my finger pointed the way, stringing the pillars together with the cables. Then I strung a cable of light from the top of pillar three to the bottom of pillar one. I did the same with pillars two and four, top to bottom, connecting them with an "X" across the rectangle. My intention was to create stability for the pillars, so I always connect them immediately. Putting the pillars in place, but leaving them unconnected from each other, creates unstable energy. I also connected all four of the pillars from the top of one, to the top of two, to the top of three, then to four and back to one. I made the same connections in the middle and bottom, then side to side and diagonally across. I began with pillar one, rotating so I didn't miss one. This completed the connection of each pillar; in "x's" from top to bottom as well as at the top, middle and bottom.

6. Next I imagined a network of smaller, one half inch cables of light growing across the "ceiling" of the new grid in uniform motion, one half of an inch apart. From the ceiling they move

down the grid walls and across the bottom. The network of cables also moved in unison throughout all of the space in each room, filling the entire home with a grid, like a loosely woven fabric, made of light. This took a minute or two. I saw this grid growing very quickly as if I was watching time lapsed film; like footage of a flower blossoming in super-fast motion. This woven network grew, spreading between all of the pillars. Each step felt nice in my body, as if I were filled with clean light.

7. After creating this kind of grid, the next step was to program the objectives into each pillar by typing them into the pillar's imaginary keyboard before activating the pillar to spin with the vibration of the program; similar to executing a computer program. I discuss how to do that step in the next chapter.

7 Activate

Thought is the sculptor who can create the person you want to be. –Henry David Thoreau

I learned to set goals as a teenager. It felt good to document my progress so I continued to set goals every subsequent year of my life. As I grew older, my goal setting skills became more explicit with excellent results. What I realized was that having goals, with a plan for achievement, was like programming myself for hitting the target. Most of the time, I achieved my objective.

Routinely I sat down to decide what I wanted to create in the coming year. Eventually I tried something new. During the last week of December, three years ago, I wrote down all the things that I wanted to experience regularly in my life: lunch with someone I love, tea with my mom and sister, reading, writing, mountain bike riding, snow skiing, waterskiing, boating, rafting, traveling, learning, adventure, friends, family, and helping others. My list did not include a job or any possessions.

At the time I wrote out the list, I worked full time. I had no idea how I was going to move into this reality, but I trusted that it could happen. With faith I took small steps toward this ideal life. Almost immediately I experienced inner calmness, less stress, joy, along with time to do what I wanted, such as write. My powerful desire to find happiness set the plan in motion with little required effort, but a lot of faith in myself and trust in the universe.

Amazing things transformed before me. As I gradually slowed down from working, income showed up from unexpected sources. Even though I couldn't see how there was income ahead of me, as long as I felt gratitude with trust, it kept working out. I kept a foot in the door of real estate much longer than I knew I should, because I didn't have as much confidence as I needed to quit completely. I worked four to eight hours a week, even though a voice inside of me said to quit completely. I couldn't quite let it go. Less income showed up from real estate no matter how many hours I put in. I kept stretching out my final leave date, not because I missed working, but out of fear of not having any income. As I struggled with the final quitting date, the universe stepped right in to make the decision for me. My business partner decided to change brokerages. At that point I had a choice to get out or get all the way back in. I knew for certain that I was not going back to real estate, so I stopped completely. It felt scary, but I made the choice to trust.

Immediately I had the best summer of my adult life. I traveled, learned, wrote, and experienced adventure after adventure. If the universe had not intervened, my summer would be void of many wonderful journeys. Within eight months of setting my goal, I no longer worked in real estate and my life consisted of the things on my list.

A goal with specific instructions works similarly to a computer program. Program your computer, alarm clock, watch, oven, or iPhone and they will follow your instructions. People follow programs as well. In America we work until age sixty five, drive on the right side of the road, say *bless you* when someone sneezes, and answer the phone when it rings due to our programming. We follow our programming unconsciously.

The programs of buildings come from the intention of those who build them and those who occupy them. Houses are programed to lodge people, provide shelter, stand firm against weather and earth movements, define space, and provide privacy. Yet we can program buildings to do much more. These huge entities have large fields of energy with many frequencies available for you to attune with *your* desires. You can encode your goals into the energy field of your home or office so that the vibrations of your goals surround you when you are indoors. The program plays like soft background music.

I recently explained this to my friend Kathy who was complaining about the uneasiness she felt in the home she rented. "You can program your home to resonate with the feelings you desire. It is simple. Businesses do it all the time. For example, a day spa wants to create a feeling of peace and relaxation. The intentions of the owners program the facility. A restaurant owner creates an inviting atmosphere so the patrons will enjoy themselves, and return often. Patrons feel invited by the owners as they walk-in."

"That's because of the beautiful décor," Kathy interrupted.

"Décor can help provide the desired aesthetics, but the intention of the owner has a greater influence. Programming the atmosphere commands a greater invitation than any objects can provide."

"I don't know how to program," Kathy commented.

"You do it all the time. When you decorated your home, to make it feel inviting, the thoughts you had while you decorate set a program into the space. You radiate your desires into the space while you perform the ritual of decorating. Instead of programming the entry of your home with the words, 'My home welcomes all who enter,' you use objects and thoughts to state your intention.

"Doesn't the decor make the person feel welcome?" Kathy asked me.

"No. Not everyone appreciates the same décor. Décor does not have the power that you do. Have you ever felt really welcomed into a place that was not well decorated?" I asked in return.

"Yes I have."

"Well, the atmosphere is what welcomed you, the intention, not the objects. Have you ever felt uncomfortable or unwelcome in a home that is well decorated?"

She nodded.

The décor affects your senses, but it's not the same as the intention in the air. If you walked into a place with your eyes closed, could you detect the vibration without the visual details of the décor? Try walking into an environment with your eyes closed. Notice how it makes you feel. Experiment in different locations.

I know firsthand that décor can only do so much. My friend Jordon and two of her associates, Kevin and Doug, decided to go into business together. Their partnership was born while the three friends sat at a local restaurant lounge consuming a few cocktails. Together they decided to begin their own lounge/dining facility.

One of Jordon's partners heard about a "good deal" on a restaurant building for sale with a liquor license. The price was about one hundred thousand dollars below market value. They made the decision to purchase the building for their new restaurant adventure. The previous owners had split up due to a personal conflict. A lawsuit ensued. The dispute included infidelity as well as other dishonesty. The building was priced to sell quickly.

However, the price was established by one of the previous partners, made with malice to hurt the other partner. Jordon's group did not concern themselves with the partners' dispute or the reason for the price reduction. They proceeded with the transaction because it was a good deal.

Jordon and her partners promptly renovated the appearance of the interior and exterior to a relaxed, inviting atmosphere with attractive décor. They created an excellent menu that included my restaurant favorite salad. They did everything correctly on a physical level.

Because one of the previous owners had not agreed to the price, he argued that he did not receive fair compensation at full market value. In an effort to recoup what he felt he was owed, he stole the liquor license from the new owners while suing his previous partners for fair compensation. During their dispute, despite Jordon's legal efforts, she now owned a restaurant which could not serve hard alcohol. This created financial stress on the business. Their business plan had depended upon the alcohol sales creating a profit. One of Jordon's partners left five months into the operation. A few months later, the other partner followed, leaving Jordon all of the responsibility and the entire financial burden. One partner had borrowed his portion of the start-up from Jordon but never repaid her. The old energy from the previous owners poisoned the new business. When purchasing the building, Jordon's group would have benefited from noticing the energy that comes with the building, and not seen only the physical appeal or lack thereof.

Their new restaurant survived for nine months before it collapsed due to the new partner disputes and financial failure. Three friends entered a business arrangement. In less than a year they parted due to unethical behaviors. The energy patterns of the previous owners lingered in the building like a musty smell not cleaned up, despite all of the new décor.

In contrast, Jake lives in the North End of Boise; a turn of the century housing area near downtown, rich in trees and squirrels. Buyers find the area especially appealing due to the ambiance, proximity to town and easy access for pedestrian and bicycle traffic. Environmentally conscious homeowners, who choose a healthy lifestyle, often are attracted to this part of Boise.

Jake and his wife decided to open a restaurant that serves healthy food choices to meet the demand of the neighborhood. They felt that the North End of Boise was a natural location. There is a small retail section in the North End where many people walk or bike for coffee or dinner. Jake chose this little niche retail place to locate his bistro. He opened a facility that served mostly organic, local food and meats from animals raised without cages. He provides superior food both in quality and taste. I love dining at his establishment. Priced a tad higher than the average, it still costs much less than the more expensive restaurants in town.

Jake demonstrates what can happen when we make our intentions clear to the universe while coming from our heart. He defined this idea clearly and chose his location based on what felt right to him. He located close to the patrons who appreciate his idea. Jake's clear intentions programmed his building to support his success. Jake owns a restaurant and knows how to place his order with the universe.

Programming requires direct, concise conviction. It feels different from asking. You would not instruct your computer, "Please do a mail merge with these addresses, if you want to, when you have time." Nor would you set your alarm clock to wake you up at "The time most appropriate for me to wake up." Each time you lack clarity, your program fails to run as intended.

I relate to the word programming really well because in college I studied computer programming, when IMB main frames were the norm and the personal computer was a new idea. I wrote in Basic and Fortran. In Fortran, I had to write the program first, then upload it to the main frame to execute it to see if it performed as intended. Many times I had to go back to the terminal to add a specific detail to the program which I had failed to include. I learned from programming computers that you must accurately convey your goal. One little comma out of place and the entire program did not work. If you forgot to close a loop, then the same function would continue forever. The universe also understands a specific language. Unclear commands do not generate the desired results.

We constantly program our life with our thoughts, words and beliefs. The words, "I am tired, or I am fat," communicate programs to run. "I am strong, I love my job, I hate my boss, I love the sun, I am healthy," also communicate to the universe. What you say to yourself and others sets a program in motion. Affirmations communicate programs. When you believe what you say, then repeat it often, you create a powerful program to convince your subconscious to execute that program. If you say each morning, "My career brings me joy and respect," eventually your subconscious will jump on board in directing you toward what it understands of career, joy and respect. It is important here to have a clear definition of what your career means to you.

I have a beautiful room in my home where I write and do healing appointments. I do yoga, read, meditate, entertain, and organize my paper-world in this space. Naturally, with my programming and goal setting background, I wanted to program this space to support my desires. I programmed the following instructions into my day room.

☐ My day room supports me in all of my personal goals with organization and harmony.

☐ I enjoy strong, healthy relationships with my family and friends that continually grow more meaningful.

☐ I contribute to world peace by creating my own inner peace and supporting peaceful activities.

Programming a room is much like programming your computer, oven or cell phone. When you set your oven to four hundred and fifty degrees, you type in the numbers, or turn the dial. You do not type into the oven "begin to get hot." You make specific instructions. When you select a ring tone on your cell phone you do not program the phone to ring "something like this one." When you order your lunch you do not tell your waiter to bring you an entrée. You communicate exactly what you want and expect to receive it. When you program a room or an entire building to support your desires, you must also state the instructions clearly. You simply need to believe that what you ordered is available on the menu.

Write your programs down before beginning to connect your home. When you are in the middle of the process, it is easy to forget the intentions as you focus on what you are doing. List your goals just the way you are going to state them, clearly and specifically. If you have a goal of increasing your income, be very specific about what it is you want. "Increased income" will not communicate a program because there are no specific details. You could say, "I add to this grid that I will double my current income of forty thousand dollars annually to eighty thousand dollars annually over the next twelve months through advertising opportunities, word of mouth, a ten percent increase in higher fees and more repeat business as well as any other ways the universe decides to create income flow for me."

When you program it into the grid of your home, feel as if it has already happened and you are enjoying your new goal. The strongest programming is emotion or feeling. Once you have decided a plan of how the income can increase, and opened your heart to accept this new program to run, then many windows will open up that you had not thought of or included in your program. But without the specific, you won't believe that it will eventually happen, nor will the program have a direction to begin running. Your details open the doors, so opportunity can flood toward you.

When I write a new program for myself, I stand up and look forward. I see an imaginary line in front of me on the floor. On my side of the line I clearly visualize myself functioning in my old program, feeling that place. On the other side of the line, I visualize and feel a different reality where my new program is running. I visualize a holographic image of myself in front of me enjoying the new program. When I feel ready, I step across the line while absorbing the new reality as a part of my current life, including taking on the feeling of living it. I feel myself accept this new reality. Then I reinforce the new reality with several confirming statements about it. For example, "I enjoy the confidence I feel knowing that my body is healthy and energized. I feel content and stress-free."

When programming your home, office or bedroom, remember these keys:

☐ Be perfectly clear about what you want. Write it down as accurately as possible.

☐ Write and state it as if it has already become a reality.

☐ Have confidence that your program will work.

☐ Set your goals from your heart center instead of your ego to avoid conflict with the will of your higher self.

☐ Feel as if it has already happened. Pretend. Fake it till you make it.

Soon you will enjoy the feeling of support from your environment as the vibrations that you wish to create are in the air around you just waiting to materialize into form.

Sometimes you can create exactly what you want, such as find the love of your life, get a great job, live in a home you enjoy, or have a loving family. Other times you put effort into being healthy and all of your efforts fail. A person might start a new business and do everything right, with no doubts of success, no dishonesty and no sabotaging behavior. They might find a building that is grounded and set the right intentions in the space. Yet despite all efforts, the business fails.

I don't know why many times you have influence over your reality and sometimes it feels as if you have none. What I have noticed is that sometimes intentions conflict with other goals. The man who wants to open a new restaurant and also spend quality time with his young children and beautiful wife has conflicting goals. A restaurant can consume a person's life, especially in the beginning years. He can't have both goals, so one goal will fail.

I have also watched people make poor choices that don't cover all of the bases to create their success. Possibly they have an agenda they haven't made known to themselves. An example of this might be a person who has an affair and doesn't know why. The affair results in a divorce and a move to another area, a new career and some dreams fulfilled that the person didn't have the courage to do without the shoe dropping and creating the opportunity.

When I set my resolution to focus on having my days filled with the peace I felt from The Reconnection, in two years following my pledge, many things fell away in my life. My career fell away. I sold my home and all of my furnishings. My income declined to a fraction of what it was, but the peace and time with family and nature increased. I found time to create from my heart, enjoy what I love to do and engage in a deeply loving relationship. I couldn't have both my career and the freedom I craved during the time I shifted into a space of learning about following my heart through a peaceful way. Many other people may have been able to keep their career and high mortgage and find their path. For me, I was lead down the path that brought me to what I valued the most, freedom to set my own agenda, outdoor recreation, quiet, nature, family and love. I didn't enjoy enough of those things with my previous work schedule. I would never trade the income I had for the abundance I enjoy now. With my new level of internal balance I pursue objects from a whole new perspective.

My friend Lisa asked me to show her how to connect her home, program two home office rooms and program her daughter's bedroom. After we connected the entire home, I showed her how to program her office. I asked her to write down her goals on a piece of paper. Then we built a grid in the room by creating pillars in the corners from floor to ceiling and connecting them with cables of light, just like we do for an entire home. We programmed her goals into each pillar and activated them.

I did this by walking over to each corner where we had built the pillars. I saw in my mind's eye a red disk at the base of each pillar. The disk had a small keyboard to accept my programs as I imagined "typing" them in and pressed a red button to activate the pillar to spin with the vibration of the program. Reading from a piece of paper, I typed into the air on the imaginary keyboard. First I said and typed into the imaginary keyboard the essentials to the grid: "I program this grid to encompass this entire home office with a grid of light, to ground to the earth and infinitely connect to all consciousness and matter. I program it to vibrate at the proper frequency to resonate with the natural earth frequencies and a frequency appropriate for the age of the structure and the use of this space." I continued, "To this grid I add Lisa's intentions that she will write a book this year, and earn sixty thousand dollars from her consulting business and have more time to relax with her family." I pushed the imaginary one inch square red button on the disk as I stated, "I activate this pillar." Then I saw and felt the pillars spinning down past the floor into the earth and up toward space away from the earth. I did the same thing with the other three pillars, stating the same words as I pretended to type.

Lastly I connected my energy with the new grid by opening my senses up to the new energy. I checked to make sure that the grid was completed and felt if the energy in the room felt better. When I was connected with the new grid in Lisa's office, I felt stronger in the space, more assured, instinctively taking a deep breath and releasing a sigh.

By doing these steps, we added what Lisa wanted to accomplish into the room so that the vibration of her goals surround her each day. Since some of her goals needed more specifics, I asked Lisa to further define them so that the program running knows exactly what to generate. Programs need explicit instructions. Lisa asked that she could concentrate in her office, be productive and generate her income from her online editing business.

Once Lisa's grid was activated, the space felt as if she had soft, encouraging words in the background supporting her to reach her goals. Today Lisa owns a company that consults and supports authors. She loves her new business and she is good at it.

Next we programmed her husband's office. He was working on designing a holistic center and new home for them on a piece of land that they owned in a nearby area. It had already been a long project with many obstacles, including challenges with city approvals and environmental issues. Two weeks after we programmed his office for clarity, focus and cooperation from the local municipalities, he reported that he experienced an easier time and momentum toward his goals.

This ritual that I use is one of many ways you can use to clearly set intentions. It is a way to mentally and emotionally effect light around you. There are many other methods you could use. Your objective is to be present with the powerful energy around you and direct it to help you with your goals.

Just as you could learn the language needed to program a computer to do all kinds of things, you can also learn the language of programming energy. We program energy all of the time, although we don't realize it. When one friend says to another, "You look great in that car. You should buy it." And the other friend replies, "There is no way I can afford this." She just wrote a program in her reality. Her words and expectations became the program.

Now you can intentionally program your life, and have a powerful grid to hold your program in place so that the vibrations of your intentions are surrounding you.

8 The Importance of the Snail Shell

Geometry existed before the creation. ~Plato

My good friend Dawn works as a real estate broker. We met fifteen years ago and became instant friends due to our similar interest in energy work. She understands the unseen world of energy and knows that it can affect us. She asked me for help during the real estate market downturn. She had several properties on the market and nothing was moving. One by one I connected a home for sale or a subdivision. The results impressed her and she asked for help with more properties. After I connected several investments for Dawn, she had some questions. She had great results in selling all of the connected properties except for one home, which took four months to find the buyer. Because of the apparent delay in the results, Dawn wanted to know more about what was involved in the process.

"I have watched you connect several locations now, and I understand most of it. But would you review the process with me so I can do this myself?" Dawn asked.

"Of course. Well, you have watched me ground and center myself, and then connect with the land and the home. Do you understand why I do that?"

"Yes, you connect to the zone and tap into your creative power. You also check-in with the land and home to see if you feel you have permission to connect the energy. Am I right?" she asked.

"You got it. And I showed you how to make a geometric shape around the home, and build pillars made of light at each corner of the shape? I said.

"Yup. Why do you make a geometric shape?"

"Geometry is the building block of the universe. The symmetry of geometry represents balance, beauty, love and wholeness. It allows the field to be balanced and harmonious. More importantly fractal geometry is the fingerprint of all patterns. Fractal geometry is like a holograph, where the smaller parts look like the greater parts and the sum or the whole looks like the smaller part."

"I haven't heard of fractal geometry. You are telling me that it is part of nature?" she asked.

"Fractal geometry is the pattern of everything. It is also called chaos theory. Chaos theory says that things that look chaotic, like the mountains, crashing waves, the stars and milky way are all measurable with a fractal formula. There is order in that appears to be chaos."

"Okay, so how does this apply to my house," Dawn replied.

"You home does not have the formula of the fingerprint of creation, the Golden Mean, Fibonacci spiral or fractal geometry. You home is designed as if several piece of the whole were gathered separately and stuck together. The cohesive math of the Golden Mean is absent and that doesn't feel healing to your body."

"Got it. Let's fix it."

"Yes, back to the pillars of light: You know that I build each pillar an equal distance above and below the surface of the land. I chose the height to be to the highest point on the structure. I'm careful that all corners and parts of the building get included, so that the grid will enclose the entire structure, right?"

"Yes, I remember that, but go over how you build a pillar again."

"I stand directly next to where the pillar will be created. I stretch out my arms around the pillar and I say in my mind, 'I create this pillar an equal distance above and below the ground, to reach the highest point on this structure:' while I breathe deeply, I see and feel the pillar of light growing from below the ground, up through my arms and to the height of the roof top or chimney top. At the same time I notice that I feel a little surge of internal light moving up through my body; a subtle but wonderful feeling."

"Ah yes, thank you," Dawn replied.

"Then I go into the middle of the home and connect all of the pillars together at the top, middle and bottom, and from the top of one to the bottom of the next and across the middle in "x's" with two inch cables of light. Remember?"

"I remember that," Dawn said nodding.

"Then I build a continuous grid between all of the pillars by visualizing smaller strings of light making a grid, connecting all of our cables and pillars together like a fabric."

"Umhum."

"Then I went to each pillar and programmed the grid with our intentions. Is that part clear?" I asked.

"Well, I don't know what I should say if I wanted to do this by myself."

"O.K. Well you can write this down if you want. I will give you an example of what to say. You must clearly state your intentions for the grid. The basic intentions connect the building to earth frequencies. The secondary intentions support the personal intentions of the occupants. The basic intentions program the light pillars to spin at the proper frequency to create a balanced magnetic field connected to the earth, bringing the Schumann Resonance into the building."

"I got that, but I want to know how I would state that?" Dawn inquired.

"Yes, I'll share that too, but I want to cover the secondary intentions next. They create the vibrations you want to add in order to support the specific goals of the occupants. Like a gentle music playing in the background. You always program in the primary intention first to connect the home to the earth's energy field. The secondary intentions follow if the occupants or owners have specific objectives they request to be programmed into the grid. If there are no goals by the owner, then there are no secondary requests. Does that make sense?"

"Yes," Dawn stated.

"For the basic intentions, I say aloud, while I type into the invisible disk; 'I program this grid to create a balanced magnetic field for this entire structure. I program this grid to create a frequency compatible with its current use and occupants. I program this grid to connect with the earth's magnetic field and the Schumann Resonance for the well-being of all who use it. I program this grid to resonate in harmony with the earth's grid to help with balance across the planet.'

"If I do not have any secondary intentions at that time, then I would say, 'I activate this grid,' while I press the imaginary red button on the disk at the ground level of the pillar. You do this same step with each pillar. Remember, a disk exists at the base of each pillar which determines the spin or frequency. When you 'type' in your program you input the information into the disk which will use the information to create the proper frequency. The disk acts similar to a computer, determining the frequency of grid."

"And if I have secondary intentions what do I say?"

"O.K., after you program in the basic intentions, instead of activating the grid, you say, 'I add into this grid the following intentions…' and you state them. Be specific. For example, if you were programming an office building where people frequently felt tired, you would specifically state, 'I add the program to this grid to bring in the energy of the Schumann Resonance to support human function and biorhythms and eliminate fatigue among the workers who occupy this structure. I further add the program to this grid to protect the occupants from exhausting, high frequency pollution from electronic and electrical equipment and wiring. I program this grid to keep toxins separate from the occupants and allow the occupants to enjoy increased energy and health.' For a specific person's request, state their name in the program. 'I program this grid to allow Sue to not be impacted by the high frequency waves and pollutants present in this building so that Sue may have ample energy to perform her work each day and feel well.' You must be clear about what you want to accomplish."

"What would you say if a secondary intention was for increased wealth for a business?" Dawn asked.

"Well, it helps to know the business needs. Let's choose a retail shop. The owner wants to increase profits. The more I know about the business needs, the better. Assuming I knew what the needs were, I would say something like, 'I program this grid to support the shop owners in finding the correct merchandise at the best possible prices to best serve the clientele who will frequent this building and shop. I program this grid that the patrons and employees will feel content, relaxed and comfortable inside this shop and will enjoy spending time here. I program this grid so that the patrons who will be best served by this retail store will learn about its location and will find time to visit the location with ease and pleasure. I program this grid so that the owners will be inspired to make any improvements to the shop to attract the most abundance possible and personal enjoyment from owning this retail store.' Does that seem specific?"

"Definitely."

"Did you notice how they specifically created a step by step process of how the shop will increase in abundance? In our world we want to have a story to explain physical manifestations. When we don't know the story, we call it a miracle and people tend to not believe it. Anytime we create a physical change, we need a story to ground it to this world so our brains will accept it. If the programmer and the occupant can both believe in the unexplainable, then I could just state, 'I program this business to thrive and triple its current profits in the next six months.' For some people that would be enough. For others, they need the story. The power for making it happen comes from the beliefs, intentions, thoughts and emotions of the people who want it. Their thoughts and emotions create the vibration of the grid even more than the words do."

"I understand that concept, but how will I think of all of that?" she asked.

"Speak from your heart what you truly want to say. Pretend that you need to give instructions to an employee and you want him to carry out this program. How would you tell him your wishes? Your program creates a vibration in the atmosphere of the building to support the intentions. The vibrations work like an encouraging friend or a song playing the tune in the background that encourages the occupants' desires. As long as you stay present while you do this, and don't let ego stop you from believing in your power, then what you are really intending will come across."

"That's awesome!" Dawn stated.

"Once you have entered the secondary intentions into the disks then activate the grid by pressing the button on the disk at the base of the pillar while stating, 'I activate this pillar.' Repeat this with each pillar. I don't bend down to the ground where the red button is. I imagine that I am pressing it with my intention. Once all of the pillars activate, then the grid vibrates with the basic and secondary intentions. The field begins to balance and strengthen. Sometimes this takes a few days or weeks to be fully balanced. Other times it happens immediately. When I am finished, I always tune into the new field to see how it feels and notice any improvements."

"But you are not done yet, right?" Dawn wondered.

"Not yet. Next I relocate myself in the center of the grid once again. While I'm centered, I spiral the energy downward into the earth in a counterclockwise motion with the intention of the spiral spinning down and outward in the pattern of a snail shell. Then I spin it upwards in a clockwise motion."

"Why the snail shell?" Dawn said puzzled.

"This is the Golden Mean. Our universe incorporates the spiral of the snail shell as part of its formation, just as it does fractal geometry. The two are intrinsically related. I can feel that relationship better than I can articulate it. Throughout nature, as well as in the shape of galaxies, and a magnetic field, this spiral pattern exists; named the Fibonacci spiral,[16] after the man who placed the mathematical calculations on the proportions of this spiral. I use it because when it spins in both directions it creates a magnetic pull and balances the magnetic field of the structure and it gives the home the energetic fingerprint that matches all of creation."

"So how do you get the energy to spin?" Dawn asked.

"I spin my body quickly for a few spins without getting myself dizzy. Then I continue the motion with my arm, using my

---

[16] http://en.wikipedia.org/wiki/Golden_spiral and http://en.wikipedia.org/wiki/Fibonacci_number

hand and index finger to point and lead the spiral. While I do this, I image the energy spinning in that direction quickly and spiraling out, sweeping wider and wider, like the snail shell. Then I repeat this going clockwise and picturing the spiral going up toward space. I feel it happening and not just image it with my thoughts. Feelings have more power than thoughts."

"What does it feel like?"

"I feel waves of clean, light energy rushing through my body bringing me peace and joy. I also feel a subtle spinning sensation that feels nice."

"Really?" she stated with a sigh.

"Yes. When I spin the energy, I feel like pure light washes over me, granting me renewed strength and vitality. I enjoy doing this process so much because of how good I feel." I explained.

"I want to try it now." Dawn paused. "Was this super easy for you to learn?"

"I wouldn't say super easy. I knew the steps and intuitively figured it out as I went along. I learned it similarly to how I learned how to help people heal themselves. I even translated some of the concepts of healing people into grounding buildings. And I got better with practice. You will too."

"Since my Broadview home did not sell right away, how do I know that the connecting really worked?"

"You will know by the way it feels. You have heard the popular buzz phrase -- *manifesting your desires,* right?" Dawn nodded. "Many newly released books address the subject. But you might focus on manifesting in the physical realm the things that you can see like a new job, home or car. This it limiting, because much of what you want you experience as feelings that you can't see, such as: love, happiness and peace. Think about it. What do you really want to manifest?"

"Health and a love life."

"Perfect. How do you know if you have manifested health or a love life?"

"Well a healthy looking body and a new boyfriend would be evidence," she smiled.

"Maybe. What about Susan Cram? She looks healthy, but she just had a full mastectomy because she had breast cancer. And what about Mike and Terra? We saw them two months ago and everything seemed fine. But now they have filed for divorced. Things are not always how they appear." I stated with an open-ended, questioning look.

"That's true."

"So, if you were able to manifest health and love, how would I know that you actually manifested it?"

"Uhm, well, I could feel if I was healthy and in love, right?"

"Yes. I'll bet that I could feel if you were as well; just like you can feel peace, even though you cannot see it." I went on to explain, "When I moved into my new home my family felt irritated with huge mood swings. After I performed the first step in connecting, my family felt much better. But, we still felt ill because the balancing was not complete. I sat quietly and learned the second process of connecting which was to spiral the energy counterclockwise and then clockwise to form the magnetic field. The end results impressed me and my family. We all felt comfortable and relaxed. You've been to my home. How does it feel to you?"

"Oh I love the way it feels."

"So you see, when you notice how something affects you, then you will know if it needs to be balanced."

"That makes sense," she concluded. "Now, do I need to understand the science behind this to make it work?"

"Definitely not! Do you understand how your car engine works before you drive your car? Not likely. You just know the few steps you need to perform to make the vehicle start and move. Do you understand the technology to operate your cell phone? Of course not. You don't need to know how it works; just that it does work. The results speak for themselves." I smiled. "You also need to believe that it works. You can manifest things that you do not see easier than you can manifest things that you do see because in the physical world you place many restrictions on how things can physically change. You don't believe that you can change your house from dirty to clean with just your thoughts. You may believe, however, that you can change how much abundance will flow to you."

"Very true. So, how does manifesting work?"

"There are many ways to put manifesting into words. You could say that your thoughts and feelings exert a *force* on unlimited pure energy. But your thoughts have to be consistent and focused to be powerful. You also need to be connected to your creative power. I call this *being in the zone*. In *the zone* you increase the power of your thoughts as you tap into All Consciousness. When you allow your heart to direct you, you create with the power of love, and thus you can create natural, healthy patterns to rewrite the script of your life's movie. Essentially you place your order with the universe," I said.

"Another way to say it is that all possible outcomes for you exist simultaneously. Whatever you believe about yourself about life, or resonate with, are the outcome that you are living. Change your beliefs, vibration, thoughts and feeling and you change your experience. Your feelings are placing your order with the universe, where all possibilities exist. Do you understand that being in the zone, one with everything, gives you the power to change energy?"

"Yes, I got that. It sounds awesome. Thank you for helping me to understand this. I'm excited to try it out."

9 Vibrations

The sound waves are vibrations, ... It's the ability to re-adjust your senses so you can feel the music."

~ David Mason

The buildings we build are built to absorb sound and vibration.

~Keith McKeown

If you have ever visited a site where many people passed away, like Auschwitz, Germany, Pearl Harbor, Hawaii or the site of the Twin Towers in New York, then you experienced that sobering feeling of utter stillness as you sense the great loss that occurred. The energy of the sadness and silence lingers there for decades or centuries.

When I visited the John F. Kennedy Memorial I looked to the familiar street scene that I witnessed on film where the public murder of an icon took place. Although President Kennedy was killed before I was born, I felt the loss through the lingering emotions of those who admired him.

Have you ridden in a car with someone that was angry and silent and then noticed that their emotion projected into the air? Even though the person looked straight ahead without speaking to you, you could feel their fury. Or have you walked into a room and felt the tension in the air? Emotional vibrations not only project out from us, but often linger around in a room or vehicle.

For three years I worked with a friend named Brian who was emotionally intense. When Brian's energy was excited, especially if he was upset, the atmosphere in our office would literally tense up, potentially making everyone uncomfortable. When Brian became cross and left a room, his energy would linger there for an hour like the smell of a skunk long after it sprayed its scent.

Like Brian, all people project vibrations that others can detect. The more power you give to emotions and thoughts, the more energy they have which can linger in a space.

When my grandmother was in her later stages of Alzheimer's, she could not speak or understand words. She didn't recognize her family members any longer, but when we sat with her, she became calmer. Without knowing who we were and without words, she relaxed as she felt the love emitting from our hearts.

Powerful emotions and intentions can hang around in a room, home or building. You can use this to your advantage by directing your thoughts, with focus, to project your desired thoughts and emotions into a room. You accomplish this by noticing the feeling you want to create in the room and giving your power to that feeling. When you do this the space will *absorb* the vibration of your energy, so you can become surrounded by the vibrations you want in your life. Imagine the results you can accomplish from directing the feelings of success into a room rather than projecting the vibration of fear.

You can also clear out emotions and thought in a structure that belonged to the previous occupants. My friend Jordon may have benefited from clearing the energy in the restaurant that she bought before she began her business. Perhaps her partnership would not have dissolved similarly to the previous owners. Much like clearing out old dirt and debris, structures need "cleaned" of old energy that does not serve the new occupants.

Once I had programmed my home to have the vibrations which supported my path, I built closer connections with people who mattered to me, something that I didn't think I had time to do before. Suddenly I had time to have tea with my mom and sister, and lunch with friends instead of only clients. I could now meditate during the day and turn my phone off for hours at a time. I checked my email to look for notes from friends, not clients and I no longer attend business events. What a relief it was to have control over my hours, my days and my life. I realized that, moment by moment, I now was choosing my experience instead of drifting along on a river without paddles. I had a motor to steer my boat and I had the delightful task of deciding where to drive this boat in flow with the river of life.

Once I became aware that my vibrations project from me

to everyone around me, I started being extra courteous when speaking to a sales clerk, server or attendant. I direct my creative power toward a pleasant, cooperative experience. By intentionally directing the experience, I avoid absorbing the energy of the other people and taking on their disposition or the energy lingering in the space around me.

People's energy can sometimes linger years after they leave. My client Rose asked me to connect the energy in her home which was built in 1902. She also asked me to see if I could clear old energy that lingered. She had her office in her home and she said that she found it difficult to focus while working. Most people would not think their environment could cause lack of focus, but your environment can have a tremendous impact on the way you feel. Often you simply need to pay attention to how the energy around you impacts you.

In one corner of her office there was a deep, narrow closet. As I approached it, an image came to me of the energy of a small girl, about six years old playing in the closet. Suddenly, the energy of the girl darted out of the closet and ran through the house. In seconds she dashed back into her favorite hiding spot. I imagined that I could talk to the little girl. In my mind I asked her to leave the home. I showed her a window right outside of the closet that she could exit through. She didn't argue or resist. She agreed to leave, but she refused the window and she raced through the home and out the front door. The picture of the little girl left my mind and the room felt calmer. Whether the energy of the little girl was real or not, my visualization felt real and the results felt real, so I trusted the image that came to me. Afterwards Rose felt more able to focus in her home office.

You can remove lingering vibrations in your home or office. This process requires you to use your imagination and trust exactly what you feel. When I teach a class on how to connect a home, I ask the students to tune into the house and the land. Sometimes we share what we noticed. Not everyone detects the same thing. A few people may pick up on the same thing, but just like interpreting a photograph, everyone will describe an image slightly differently. Just trust exactly what comes to you and imagine that you can change it at will. Remember that your intuition, which may be coming from your right hemisphere, sees things in pictures, not language.

As you trust yourself to change the energy in the way that it feels good to you, feel your way through the process of how to make the change, then allow the change. If I feel that I will need to imagine a rainstorm coming into a home to wash all of the negative energy out of the home, then I will trust that. I will imagine the rain pouring over everything; washing the walls, air and objects clean of old vibrations.

Occasionally I run into a situation that won't change. I trust that too. While programming a sixteen year old girl's room one time, I noticed an energy hiding in her closet. I approached the energy and tuned into it. I felt the presence of a young, timid boy about the age of twelve. I asked him to leave and he refused. I insisted that he leave and he refused again. Then the energy begged me to allow him to stay. He explained that he liked to hide in this closet because it was the only place he felt completely safe. He promised that he meant no harm. I felt that I couldn't push him out, so I mentioned the experience to the girl. She said, "Is that why I always feel like someone watches me in my closet?" I didn't know how to respond. But she claimed that she didn't mind him staying there. I programmed her room with her goals. She experienced an easier time in school and increased focus.

Use your imagination and trust the fun process like a game. See what happens. In the worst case, nothing happens. The best results are clear energy ready for new imprinting.

Like emotions, all things vibrate, including buildings. Even the energy in the rooms in buildings vibrates. Like the anger which lingers in the air, the vibrations in the air in your home can affect you. Initially the vibrations in my home made my family irritable. Halfway through the balance process we felt flu-like. When the home was completely balanced, we felt safe, supported and well.

Now you can program the space around you to create the vibrations you want to feel. If you can clearly imagine your perfect life, happy, abundant, in harmony with others, surrounded by loving people, or whatever life you want to create, then you have already mastered step one to creating it. But how will you feel in your ideal life? Decide how you want to feel, and program those vibrations into your grid.

Remember the key steps to program the vibrations around you:

1.   Visualize clearly how you will feel when you have your new goals. Then feel that you already have them. Feel the emotions as often as you can throughout the day.

☐   Example: I love where I live.

2.   Imagine that you experience the feeling along with gratitude for experiencing it.

☐   Example: I feel gratitude for my home. I am blessed to live in a place I enjoy so tremendously.

3.   Choose words and actions that support the way you already feel.

☐   Example: I share with all my friends and family my appreciation. I take very good care of my home and share its pleasant atmosphere with loved ones. I care for my home with respect.

4.   Program your environment to support your desired vibrations.

☐   Example: I program this home to emit the vibrations of love, happiness and gratitude so that I feel love and peace in my home.

5.   Maintain the focus on how you want to feel.

☐ Example: I trust the universe to lead me to where I need to be. My heart feels content where ever I live. Unlimited options abound. I am grateful.

These techniques allow you to surround yourself with the vibrations you wish to feel. No longer will the vibrations in atmospheres of structures affect you in ways that don't support you because you can change them. You can take command of your environment today to direct it to support your path. You have an army of energy around you at your command. Now you must direct the army.

Exercise: Spend time in nature listening, appreciating and respecting her beauty. Say something pleasant to wildlife. Take a lost bug outside instead of squishing it. Think about another area of the world which is connected to your home through earth's chi. Notice how your environment is making you feel, both in nature and in structures.

10 Volcanoes Be Still

...there is throbbing through the Earth, energy available everywhere, (that) would enable man to dispense with the necessity of mining, pumping, transporting and burning of fuels, and so do away with innumerable causes of waste!
~Nicola Tesla,

Tesla gave us the radio, alternating electric current, remote control, hydropower and much more. A Nebraska born Native American, called Blue Thunder, shares a common understanding with one of the greatest inventors of the twentieth century.

I arrived at the local park searching for someone I knew. The scene was alive with Frisbees, dogs and the laughter of children. I noticed a group of people sitting against the hillside with a couple of drums and rattles. Instinctively I walked toward them. Several familiar and friendly faces came into focus, some of whom I wasn't expecting. Standing in front of the group, the speaker stood out from the rest. His blue neoprene headband held his brown, shoulder-length locks in place. Wearing a loose fitting, hippy-style short sleeve shirt, baggy denim pants and around his neck he wore a Native American necklace with eagle claws, he looked like a man bridging two cultures, worlds apart.

This unassuming, freckled Shoshone Elder captured my heart as quickly as my attention. I slipped quietly into the seated group of twenty or so people and listened intently to the words of wisdom offered.

Sitting on the grassy hillside at Camel's Back Park, facing the evening May sun, I noticed that he appeared to be in his mid-forties. He carried himself like a young elder with great wisdom to share with all who would listen. He stood barefoot in the cool grass explaining that he traveled the northwest with his drum in hand sharing the stories of the awakening of humanity. He expressed his message of hope in a gentle, caring manner with deep passion. From dreams, visions and native traditions, he knew Mother Earth intimately. As he spoke, quiet stirring swirled within my being. He told us of the great Sun and Mother Earth. I felt his message as a powerful story of our connection to earth and each other. He called people the red skinned, brown, white and yellow skinned and spoke of us all joining to become one people. He said that representing fire was the white skinned, the soil; the red skinned, water; the brown skinned, and air or wind; the yellow skinned. As we come together, we would reunite the elements of the planet, creating a wholeness of human spirit, fully connected.

He spreads the vibration of joy as he beats his drum which resonates with the heartbeat of our Great Mother, sending his loving thoughts out in waves with each strike.

I listened attentively as he told us the story of Yellowstone National Park and how his message of hope brought healing to that area. Blue Thunder explained that in 2006 disappointing reports surfaced from seismologists that for nearly twenty months the volcanic and seismic activity below Yellowstone National Park, as well as a number of related northwest mountains, was building. Experts warned of possible eruptions of one of the world's largest super volcanos. The earth whispered to Blue Thunder that the area was out of balance. Immediately he went into action. Within months he organized a group activity including building a giant healing crystal medicine wheel.

The activity was announced through word of mouth and the internet. Time was of the essence as the underground volcanic activity increased steadily. Nearly one hundred people gathered, with several cultures represented, joining Blue Thunder as he built the large medicine wheel of crystal and local vegetation. With drumming, singing and dancing in Yellowstone National Park, he sent out love from his heart in order to bring peace and balance to twelve northwest mountains. He beat his drum from sunup to sundown for two days. With faithful conviction Blue Thunder projected out love, vibrating calmness with the beat of his drum while others added their loving vibration and song.[17]

---

[17] June 2008 - Blue Thunder gathered in the Teton Mountains to bring needed peace to the mountains once again.

Blue Thunder quieted the mountains with his understanding that we all are one with each other, the animals and the planet. What we feel internally is expressed in our external world. When Blue Thunder felt love and peace, it reflected back to him from the surrounding earth.

I realized that he had done the same thing I did with my home, only he used a very different technique. I was present with the earth, my home and the universe to become fully conscious that everything is already connected. Blue Thunder connected himself with the volcano, and land and the universe to resonate the universal vibration of love. I used imaginary pillars, spirals, love and appreciation and grids of light. He used his drum, his voice, crystals, plants and his love, respect and appreciation for nature. Blue Thunder and I merged our consciousness with everything; as if we were clouds of energy dripping our awareness like raindrops to touch all that exists, seeing everything as one, which it already was.

This shows that the technique is just a tool to get the result of making the connection between human, earth and structures. There are many techniques that you could use. The one I teach in this book is the one that works for me. As I mentioned earlier, there will be a time when you become more familiar with how powerful you are as creators. When that occurs, you will make these connections simply by being fully present and grounded to the earth while you connect your magnetic field to a structure or place on the planet. By doing this you recognized that the energy was already connected as one, but without conscious recognition.

That night in the park, I studied his face carefully as Blue Thunder brought his attention into his heart to connect with unlimited love for infinite possibilities. His face grew calm as his breath slowed. He lifted his chin, exposing his throat and pushing his chest forward as if doing so allowed his heart and throat to open up enough to touch everything around him. I felt his powerful connection and friendship with all people, living things and the earth as he spoke of offering respect to all and allowing everything to be as it is. Like Blue Thunder, your access to boundless love never ceases. No matter who you are, you've always been infinite love and never-ending energy, able to direct the vibration around you.

In 2005 Blue Thunder offered to assist with the droughts of northern Utah and southern Idaho. The Bear Lake area had experienced twenty years of falling water levels above and below ground. The deficiency was so severe that the trees in the mountains were dying from lack of moisture and Bear Lake dropped fifteen feet from its normal level. The area was heavy with mountain mining and damage to the flow of earth energy. Lack of respect for nature caused an imbalance.

Blue Thunder looked at the maps and drew a grid on the map, called a medicine wheel, around the area that needed harmonized. This wheel had several mountain points along its rim. He visited the mountain points along the medicine wheel bringing his drum, crystals, sage and intentions to send out the vibration of love with each beat of his drum. Blue Thunder came to the area to send love, harmony and restore balance from careless mining or other causes that lacked harmony.

The healing followed quickly. Blue Thunder visited the small, mountainous community and the snow began to fall. Two feet fell the night of his first ceremony. Blue Thunder returned a month later to do a second ceremony. Again two feet of snow fell. By that following spring the lake recovered to its normal level, rising fifteen feet, ending a twenty year drought. Several local townspeople were so moved and impressed by the success of Blue Thunder that they made a movie about his journey there. You can watch this incredible film and see how the town of Bear Lake thanks Blue Thunder for creating the second wettest winter in history. The lake was 17.5' below normal and the lake rose to full in that one winter following Blue Thunder's visit. [18]

In the movie they ask him, "How do you make the weather bring us the rain we've lacked for twenty years?"

Blue Thunder said in essence, 'I send out love to the area with my intention and I beat my drum to reverberate it outward.

---

[18] Documentary on how Blue Thunder helped Yellowstone and Bear Lake. http://www.youtube.com/watch?v=4WEVY41EpKq

What is in my heart heals her. She can feel the devotion and respect to resonate again with love, which is the vibration of the universe.'

Blue Thunder understood what Tesla did; that "energy exists everywhere." You can do what Blue Thunder and I do to connect and heal the earth. You can connect yourself with this energy by using your focus to become one with it. You are the force that merges it together again. You gather the light of the prism and show the world that it is one stream of light and only appears to be refracted into pieces.

Blue Thunder further awakened the part of me that can sense the energy of all objects, land and people. After meeting Blue Thunder, my confidence in the power of the light within me grew stronger. If he could quiet volcanoes by uniting the energy, I knew that I could balance the energy in a home or maybe even an area. Blue Thunder's words and success inspired me to try my connecting grid on a larger scale. I have witnessed Blue Thunder and others send their musical vibration to the outer world like a silent song of love which touched everything around them. Blue Thunder showed me that he could affect the weather and calm volcanoes. It is similar to what Dr. Masaru Emoto [19] does when he heals water with intention and love through words and thoughts. His books and photographs of the changes made to water, inspire many and show visually how powerful our thoughts are on effecting our environment.

Blue Thunder's great respect and appreciation for nature reawakened my deep connection with the flora and fauna, which began at a very young age when I learned to love the outdoors. As an Idaho native, I appreciated spending time surrounded by the tempo of Mother Earth, which comforted me like a familiar blanket. The sunrise and sunset communicated to me the creativity and wonder of this amazing planet. The forest sang to me in rhythmic pulsation, a music where the breeze danced with the plants and trees. Animals, insects and birds all harmonize in sound to soothe my body. My childhood was full of long walks in the forest, fishing on a river bank or watching the deer graze from my front window. Nature always calmed me.

Many times doubt would swell up inside of me about the truth of reconnecting buildings to earth's energy. When doubt would grow strong, I would think of Blue Thunder, the one man who could quiet volcanoes and make water return to a barren land. I would remember his words about the sun, the heartbeat of

---

[19] Shows how water responds to words, pictures, thoughts, and intention. http://www.masaru-emoto.net/english/water-crystal.html

124

the earth, and the gathering of all the people, white, red, brown and yellow. His enlightened message reminded me of how the natural world speaks to me and I speak back. Although my technique is far different from his, my intention for harmony is the same. He used the words love, harmony and vibration. I use the words balanced magnetic energy field programmed with the intention of harmony. They really mean the same thing.

Build a Giant Grid on 160 acres of land

I never met the farmers who toiled, tilled, sowed, harvested and sweated on this 160 acre piece of land for hundreds of years to create nourishing food for sale. How many generations the land passed from family member to family member I knew not. It seemed apparent that appreciation was given to the land with the understanding that it would produce healthy crops from respect and proper care; even love and appreciation.

This land was impacted when our government and central banking system decided to stimulate the growth of our national economy. I was actively participating in one of the largest industries; real estate. They made money easy to borrow to encourage investment and spending. A developer I knew met with a national bank who promised him loans for a subdivision, so he searched for land. He found one hundred and sixty acres that grew crops, which left the skilled developer seeing dollar signs as he envisions housing growing out of the ground as quickly as corn.

I remember when engineers, city council and planning and zoning members signed their names, giving the experienced man permission to grow a crop of track housing.

Two years later, well into the project, the economy begins to contract due to the stimulation of a false expansion. Or maybe the banks that run the world create false contraction in order to build their empire. Regardless, the developer was left with a half-grown crop of homes and money draining out of his pocket every day. The debts piled high and the contraction of money grew tighter.

The marketing team for the subdivision became stressed from the pressure they received by the developer, who was pressured by the bank. My good friend Amy knew that I could improve energy. She approached me to "fix" the subdivision as the economy took its toll. In this subdivision, sales had stopped completely for the past three months.

"Amy, I don't know if connecting the subdivision to the earth's grid will help your sales. That's not the purpose of what I do. I connect the vibration between earth and people. It has nothing to do with profits."

"Okay. I understand. But when you connect a house or land then it feels better to people, right?" Amy asked.

"Yes, it feels better to people because our bodies like to be in harmony with the earth's natural rhythms."

"Right. Right. So, if you connect this subdivision, then people will like the way it feels out here, and they will want to live here. It might work."

"It might, but that's not what I'm here to do. I'm here to help people connect with the planet."

"Exactly, what better way to help people than to connect a subdivision? All of the people who live here will feel more connected. See, you are doing your work."

I thought about her logic. Maybe this was a great way to help people. The question was, could I summon the quiet focus I would need to connect one hundred and sixty acres of land? I didn't know the answer. I didn't know how I was going to do it. Up to this point I had only connected a few homes; nothing on a large scale like an entire neighborhood.

"It can be done," I felt inside my body.

The housing bubble showed signs of bursting in Boise late in 2006. By midway through 2007 the real estate market crash was gradually beginning nationwide. Prior to the crash, Boise was in the top three fastest growing cities in the nation. That quickly changed to a five to eight year supply of real estate on the market.

I was still new at connecting homes and buildings, but I found it healing for myself. I assumed that the more property I connected, the more harmonious people and the planet would feel. I watched Blue Thunder heal large areas of land, extending his healing vibration for hundreds of miles. With Blue Thunder for inspiration, I accepted the quest to harmonize the acres dotted with some newly occupied homes and some vacant ones.

During the fourteen years I had known Amy, she always encouraged me to further my intuitive gifts. Few people knew my healing powers more intimately than she.

Fourteen years earlier, on the day that she and I met, it took about ten minutes for us to become instant friends. The first two minutes were spent sizing each other up for competition. It took only seconds to make the friendship after we let our guard down. We spent that night talking and doing intuitive work until 6:00 am. I used my sensitive powers to read Amy's body energy that first night. When I touched her arms, in my mind I could see Amy crossing her forearms tightly over her stomach terrified of fire as a small child. I asked her, "Amy, where was the fire when you were about five years old? I can feel that you have a fear of fire, but it was not at your home. Where was it?" Amy was quiet as she reflected back to her youth searching for a fire.

"The only thing I can think of is that when I was five years old I was camping with my family. A lady in the camp next to us poured gasoline on her fire and she was burned to death. My father and I walked over to her campsite and looked down on her charred body. All I could think was, 'I hope that never happen to me.'"

"Oh my gosh, Amy, that's horrible. Can you imagine how that would impact a five year old?"

Amy and I spent a few minutes in the wee hours of the morning to clear the trauma from her body. She was so impressed with my skill that she trusted my intuition and ability to feel energy ever since. Many times she asked me to diagnose her son's hand or injury for broken bones, to know if she needed to take him to the doctor. She has been my number one cheerleader, having more confidence in my intuitive skills than even I did.

With her trust in my abilities, we ventured out to build a magnetic energy field around one hundred and sixty acres together. We made it fun. I decided to use mandalas (colorful symmetrical patterns within a circle) and small natural stones the color of the rainbow and our seven major chakras[20] to symbolize wholeness. These items were for our benefit of showing our intentions and were not necessary to make a light grid.

I began at the corner of the property on the left side of the main entrance. I placed a few stones and a mandala two inches below the soil at the base of each pillar. Amy poured purified water on the symbols. The symbols solidified our intention in our own beings, but they were not what made the magic happen.

---

[20] https://en.wikipedia.org/wiki/Chakra

With my mind I imagined a pillar one hundred feet tall and ten feet in diameter while standing in front of it at each of the four corners of the subdivision, to support this extensive grid. The third corner was only accessible by walking down a canal road about half a mile. About six hundred feet from the corner, a blue heron appeared in front of us on the narrow road. At first we stopped to enjoy the grace of this magnificent bird, but as we continued down our path, the blue heron lead the way. It walked in front of us about one hundred feet. When we finally arrived at the property's corner, the beautiful bird remained ahead of us on the road to oversee our activity. When we were finished he simply flew away. For whatever reason the bird seemed to be supportive and approving, like a guardian angel.

Once four magnificent energy pillars were in place at the four corners, I connected them with large cables of light, making "x's" and connected them all top, middle and bottom. Then I programmed Amy's and my intentions into the newly formed grid.

The results were impressive. Connecting this subdivision created a huge shift. Sales increased immediately. The entire phase was sold-out in a matter of six months. This impressed both Amy and me, considering the local and national housing market. One might believe that the grid had tremendous influence, but in truth the power came from us. We used the grid as a tool to direct our power.

My healing skills were growing, from affecting my own emotions and health, to creating things I wanted to happen in my life, including connecting my home and improving the energy around a one hundred and sixty-acre subdivision. My confidence in my intuitive, sensitive nature was expanding. My ego of course still wondered if I was making the whole thing up. But I decided, *my entire experience is created by me. And so, what more can I create? What can't I do?* I saw no limit.

Every person has the same ability to develop their intuitive skills. My goal is to share this knowledge with you so you can trust your inner knowing, develop your imagination, and realize your full potential. When you do this you can find your individual gifts to contribute to the world.

I continued to trust my intuition and do what I loved every day. I kept meditating. Eventually I learned to meditate with my eyes open, which turned out to be the same experience as living in the moment. Once I learned how to do that, the doors flew open tall and wide. Life became a series of rushing, euphoric pleasures.

I began to notice things that I had never noticed before, even though I had done them hundreds of times. I could feel the shampoo spilling onto my skin, how smooth it felt as I rubbed my hands together to spread the creamy liquid evenly, enjoying the sensation. My fingers ran the goo through my hair and the suds took shape, bubbling between my fingers, thick and fluffy in my mane.

While standing in my shower, full of suds in my hair, I looked out the shower window and saw the sun hitting the hillside across the street. Rocks and sagebrush sporadically broke-up the hillside of wild grass. The pine trees in my yard sparkled in the morning light. I breathed in deep and let out a sigh. I couldn't imagine a more peaceful way to begin my morning; standing under warm flowing water, watching the beautiful morning light spread across the untamed land before me.

That afternoon, as I sat on my patio taking a break from writing, the sunlight's low position in the sky hit various places on a healthy aspen tree, leaving some leaves dark green and others glowing brightly. The trunk was spotted with dark and light areas. Birds flittered all around, calling loudly in a language that I didn't speak. A light blue/grey butterfly bounced along a few inches from the ground. The sun warmed me, while the light breeze cooled my feet. I never felt the breeze quite so distinctly or heard the individual call of the birds so musically.

I had learned to be present and enjoy the moments. Yet there was more to learn.

11 Starting Right

The significant problems we face in life cannot be solved at the same level of thinking we were at when we created them. Albert Einstein

Earth is what we all have in common.

Wendell Barry

For three thousand years Eastern mystics created a balance between humans and Earth with the use of feng shui by merging the physical structure with spiritual intentions. Sites were carefully selected to complement structures with nature. Indigenous cultures asked the elements and land if this was a wise place to build or dig, and they surveyed the area to minimize their impact on wildlife, vegetation and natural waterways. Buildings were not constructed primarily for the builder's income, but with thoughtful consideration for both physical and spiritual purposes.

When developments and buildings are constructed without respect for humans and the planet, a vibration of conflict and disharmony is created. Blue Thunder explains that when we dig a hole in the earth without respect for her, then light and energy bleed from her, similarly to when we have a wound on our bodies. This causes energy imbalances. He further explains that the earth can be sick or have cancer in areas due to poor health from mistreatment. There are many places on the earth where we see fish dying, polluted waters, toxic soil and dying vegetation. Earth's problems belong to us. We cause them and it affects us in return.

Subdivisions and buildings hold frequencies. They resonate with their surroundings, absorbing the thoughts and sentiments of the individuals who built them and the populace who frequent them. Aggravated words, physical cruelty, selfishness and other harmful sentiments can linger in a room, building or neighborhood, affecting the inhabitants, community and the earth. Harmful energy, such as fearful or self-serving thoughts have a definite impact on the flow of chi in a dwelling or area. Damaging the soil and water during construction can have a lasting impact.

For builders and developers, profits become the fundamental factor in construction, and often consideration for nature loses its priority. Ponds, trees and creatures are destroyed or displayed without a second thought. Grave sites, sacred sites and beautiful natural resources are taken without permission and destroyed, or their life-force disturbed enough to create tumultuous swirls of confused energy with no place to go.

Architects and Engineers

A number of engineers and architects consciously design in harmony with the earth. They bring a higher vibrational quality into their work which benefits the people who occupy the spaces. These places draw people to them. Natural light, low impact on the earth and pleasant, harmonious frequencies make people feel good and enjoy being in the structure.

Respect for all creation unlocks the door to a beautiful future. Opposing respect is an attitude of, *look out for number one without regard for the greater good*, which often leads to trampling over precious life. Appreciation for the planet coincides with self-respect. The amount on one side of the scale equals the other.

What does harmony with the environment look like? William McDonough[21] can tell you about sustainable living in his book *Cradle to Cradle*. One of the most well-known architects of green building design, McDonough believes in making our world

---

[21] In 1996, McDonough received the Presidential Award for Sustainable development. In 2003, he earned the first U.S. EPA Presidential Green Chemistry Challenge Award. In 2004, he received the National Design Award for environmental design.

beautiful by designing beautiful homes and office buildings with the idea of reuse/recycle all material. The earth recycles and renews as it breaks down waste and creates life from the nutrients left behind.

The principles of excellent architecture are balance, symmetry, beauty and function. Unfortunately, society focuses on the price tag more than harmony, opting for quantity over quality. Aesthetics are compromised to save a few dollars, with ultimately greater costs.

As I mentioned earlier, my daughter wrote her thesis on creating attractive low-income housing. She states that dilapidated buildings break people's spirit. When a building lacks maintenance, pride and respect fade. This affects the human psyche.

Surrounded by beauty, we develop inner peace. As my architect friend Ryan says, "Beautiful buildings last because people do not tear down well-built, attractive buildings." We tear down ugly, poorly constructed ones.

As humanity grows in its capacity for love and self-respect, love extends to all of humanity, the planet and the structures. With respect firmly in place, we begin to shift our focus from a cost driven society to one driven by beauty and harmony. This requires our collective awareness to open up to abundance for all and let go of the fear that there is not enough money, resources, or time.

The masses must take action to create this shift. Free energy to all the world has been invented several times during the last sixty years. This technology would provide free energy to the entire world, opening up opportunities to abundance for all people. The wealthiest people in the world have a conflicting interest with allowing abundance around the globe, so they have confiscated machines that provide electricity free of wiring and cars that run without petroleum. As a collective, it is our responsibility to demand that money hungry giants not control the world's assets to gain full power of the planet. We must share the earth wisely and respect her gifts or she will be depleted of health and resources.

Architects and engineers lead our quest for a more beautiful future. Conscious designs appeal to more customers as humanity shifts in awareness. The ultimate building design circulates a balanced electromagnetic energy field so the building harmonizes with the earth's resonant frequencies; which is also humanity's resonant frequencies. When buildings' high frequencies interrupt the flow of chi around the Earth, it creates an unhealthy planet and can make our structures weak and more susceptible to decay.

Additionally, architects can:

- Recognize the needs of the natural surroundings on the land around buildings
- Provide ample internal airflow

- Protect people from exposure to high frequency waves
- Provide natural light

Builders and Developers

Builders can contribute by building well designed homes that respect the land and environments during construction. They can go further by recycling materials, taking care to prevent pollution of a site, using energy efficient materials, as well as becoming educated on alternative, environmentally friendly products. For example, in California there are entire subdivisions built with leased solar panels. The residents pay a monthly leasing fee which costs about the same as electric utility bills. Builders can incorporate solar without increasing the purchase price. More natural materials are available. Some carpets on the market are harmless to human bodies if ingested. That doesn't mean we eat the rugs when food is low, but it means that they don't have harmful chemicals like most carpeting. Some residents of new construction experience serious health issues from heavy chemicals in new home materials.

A home already connected to natural frequencies will appeal to more buyers. Buyers spend more time viewing a home they feel comfortable in. They purchase a home that makes them feel good. This translates into greater sales for conscious builders. Reverence for the environment reflects self-respect. Earth is our home.

Developers can design subdivisions to support the environment. In my subdivision the covenants require that I landscape a percentage of the yard with sod grass, which is not friendly to our high desert environment. Lawn mowers produce much higher emission pollution than cars do. Lawns require water, fertilizer and weed killers; harmful to the environment. I wish that my developer would open up to new possibilities, allowing for alternative green ground covers, including edible landscape such as thyme and native plants. Developers and engineers can focus on creating beauty in all price points of developing without damage to nature in order to minimize the impact on wildlife.

Consumers

Consumers can choose to pay for beautiful, earth conscious designs by voting with their dollars for friendly products. They can seek energy efficient designs and products.

Government

Governments can also make balance a part of their theme. With creative minds, tax payers save money in the long run with beautiful, efficient buildings. Tax payers save money when buildings last longer. Increased productivity, from healthy workers, benefits the whole country.

Governments around the world can also begin to support the technology that is kind to the earth. Government can support research to explore Nicola Tesla and other inventors that claim there is free energy for everyone. They claim that a machine can literally pull enough electricity out of the air or the earth to run appliances and equipment. But this technology is not in the best interest of large industries. Big businesses have hidden advancements in medicine, oil-alternative energy and organic food production[22] from the market because earth friendly products don't help their bottom line. These same companies pay the government to give them a competitive advantage over consumers. The human race won't be at peace until we care about what is in the best interest of the whole.

Business Owners

Business owners can benefit by creating environments where patrons want to visit while at the same time reducing the businesses impact on the earth. To help create what you want your business to be, set your intention by programming goals into a grid; such as your desired gross sales, availability of products, the right employees and access to your target customers. Balancing an environment strengthens the integrity of the building's structure, the infrastructure and the equipment in the facility. In the long run this requires less long-term maintenance.

---

[22] Just one example is Monsanto who is hiding the fact that production diminishes for farmers within a couple of years due to damage to the soil and their crops require a greater amount of Roundup each year to kill weeds.
http://thestateweekly.com/the-organic-review-new-study-shows-monsanto-claims-on-yields-environment-are-false/
and http://www.huffingtonpost.com/2013/05/31/europe-monsanto-gmo-crops_n_3367284.html

This means not dumping toxic waste into the waters, being conscious of how products are made and being careful to preserve and respect the planet and the well-being of workers. It means fair compensation and flexibility for family needs, health and no mandatory overtime. When a business compromises their employees and nature, the damage goes far beyond the walls and reach of the business. It affects the whole earth.

Many owners already created the energy needed to accomplish all of this just with their intentions and actions. They perform a few rituals to express their intentions, i.e. ground breaking ceremonies, dedication prayers, or they balanced it through Feng Shui or decorating. Owners can take it one step further by connecting the buildings that feel out of balance to equalize the building's frequencies with our planet and help harmonize the frequencies around the globe. They can also make a commitment to construct new buildings to resonate with the natural rhythms.

Offices and factories are some of the worst environments for humans. If a living, green plant cannot thrive in the building, than neither can a human. We are animals and we are part of nature. Workers need direct or indirect sunlight, fresh air, clean water and the Schumann Resonance. Ideally, plants or running water should be included indoors to give fresh oxygen and calm the nervous system.

Mother Nature is sacred and alive. She must be treated with love and respect for our well-being as well as hers. Today we are starting to get the message. Some builders and architects are consciously designing in harmony with the Earth, and the results are heavenly: they truly bring a higher vibrational quality into their work.

Today, we are all becoming aware that energy must flow through every part of our lives. There are so many ways that we can increase the flow of chi within and around our planet. We are beginning to clean up toxins, keep our water and air clean and cease using harmful chemicals on the Earth and in our bodies. New buildings are being constructed with natural materials that work in harmony with the environment and create sustainable communities. Many are living in love and peace. Others connect with the planet by honoring Nature.

These changes help, but they will also take time for the masses to implement. This is why connecting a building is so valuable. It is something all of us can do right now. Each time you connect a building to resonate with Earth's rhythm, you are shifting the vibration to help people, their structures and the planet. You are helping life-force energy to travel through structures unimpeded, continuing the flow and allowing sunlight's healing infrared rays to penetrate the earth's surface and mend her wounds. When our structures vibrate with the

Earth's natural geomagnetic and electromagnetic fields, we are supported in maintaining that natural state of being for ourselves.

A Challenge to You: Make a personal commitment of what you will do to make buildings more compatible with the planet: i.e. reconnect your home, purchase an earth friendly home, design an earth friendly home, or educate others about how the earth's rhythms affect us and our health.

For one-on-one coaching to Harmonize your Home or Office, Contact Diana Anderson at diana@dianaanderson.com

About the Author

Diana learned at an early age the power of intuition and her sensitivities to the unseen world. Through touch, she was able to feel the physical pain of others beginning at age seventeen. Through extensive research and training, she has honed her intuitive skills. Today she healings other through The Reconnection as well as through healing touch. Building and land also receive her healing love when needed.

In addition to her healing work, she works with couples, helping them develop deep connections and bonds that come through open-heart intimacy.

She also writes romantic fiction under a pen name, Karen Diana Montee. You can find out more about her work at www.diana-anderson.com

Other books include:
- Painted with Love (a novel)
- Your Secret Chamber
- Always in the Mood
- Deep Sex
http://www.amazon.com/-/e/B00AQ5P61W

www.ingramcontent.com/pod-product-compliance
Lightning Source LLC
Chambersburg PA
CBHW060507030426
42337CB00015B/1782